What people are saying about *Peace in the Hood*...

"With *Peace in the Hood*, Aquil Basheer and co-author Christina Hoag give a unique and heroic memoir that has the blood-haunted and thrilling narrative immediacy of David Simon's *The Wire* while also providing an inspiring real-world primer that shows how residents of the nation's most violence-damaged communities learned techniques to interrupt the insidious cycle of gang retaliation, thus starting the healing process for their communities.

"*Peace in the Hood* is a compelling read for all, and a must-read for law enforcement, mayors, lawmakers, and anyone else interested in curing the dual toxicities of violence and mass incarceration that plague America's most vulnerable neighborhoods."

— Celeste Fremon, author of *G-Dog and the Homeboys*
Editor/founder of WitnessLA.com and The California Justice Report

"*Peace in the Hood* is a must-read for anyone engaged in violence prevention and community building. Beyond its importance as a blueprint for change, this is also the story of a hero whose devotion to peace exemplifies the servant leader."

— Jorja Leap, PhD, adjunct professor, UCLA Luskin School of Public Affairs

"Aquil Basheer's extensive experience addressing violence through community mobilization and street outreach has been exceptionally valuable to our work here in Seattle. As a result of his training, mentoring, and support, our street outreach team has significantly improved its operations through standardization, protocols, and preparation. Harder to measure but equally important has been the team's increased confidence and sense of belonging to an extensive peer network dedicated to working for peace in some of the country's toughest neighborhoods. *Peace in the Hood* allows these lessons to be shared more broadly.

— Mariko Lockhart, director
Seattle Youth Violence Prevention Initiative, City of Seattle

"The information in *Peace in the Hood* is invaluable and, if used, can change destructive communities across the nation into healthy, violence-free safe zones. What Aquil Basheer and his program have done for me has been miraculous, turning a once hardcore former street soldier like myself into a refined, respected professional with structure, discipline, accountability. A big ups to him and his program.

— Reno Williams, community violence interventionist
Former gang member and prison inmate

"The Professional Community Intervention Training Institute has been a vehicle of change in Los Angeles, ground zero for gang and gun violence in the U.S. The Institute works to prevent violence by understanding its nature and thereby helping to create safe, healthy neighborhoods."

— Julio Marcial, program director, The California Wellness Foundation

"PCITI stands alone in its ability to educate and train qualified ex-gang members to become valued peacekeepers in their neighborhoods. While each of these men and women have respect in their communities, Aquil and his team transform them into professionals who can survive on the street, work with law enforcement, and save lives. Aquil is completely selfless in his chosen path of making Los Angeles and the world a safer place and allowing children to pursue their goals and dreams."

— Bob Hoff, board member, A Better LA

"The Professional Community Intervention Training Institute is one of the best things I ever did. It's something I'm proud of. It really helped me become a man. Since I graduated from PCITI, I've been on a roll."

— Anthony Porter, community violence interventionist
Former gang member

"Aquil Basheer's commitment to our communities is telling through his steadfast leadership in the field of community-violence reduction. His approach is one that promotes empowerment through his established trainings that seek to strengthen community members to successfully sustain peace and end conflict."

— Robert Hernandez, adjunct assistant professor
School of Social Work, University of Southern California

"Aquil Basheer has helped to raise awareness and amplify community-based gang intervention as a central component to any public safety plan. His work, which is informed by his personal experience over forty years and is practitioner driven, sustains peaceful and healthful communities."

— Mike de la Rocha, advisor on criminal justice issues to Congressman Tony Cardenas

peace in the HOOd

Working with Gang Members to End the Violence

AQUIL BASHEER

AND

CHRISTINA HOAG

An imprint of
Turner Publishing Company

Turner Publishing Company
424 Church Street • Suite 2240 • Nashville, Tennessee 37219
445 Park Avenue • 9th Floor • New York, New York 10022
www.turnerpublishing.com

Library of Congress Cataloging-in-Publication Data
Basheer, Aquil.
Peace in the hood : working with gang members to end the violence / Aquil Basheer,
Christina Hoag ; foreword by Pete Carroll.
pages   cm
Includes index.
ISBN 978-0-89793-704-7 (paperback)—ISBN 978-0-89793-706-1 (spiral)
ISBN 978-0-89793-705-4 (e-book)
1. Gangs—United States—Case studies.   2. Gang members—Rehabilitation—United States.
3. Youth and violence—United States.   I. Hoag, Christina.   II. Title.
HV6439.U5B384 2014
364.106'60973—dc23   2014015263

Project Credits

Cover Design: Brian Dittmar Graphic Design	Managing Editor: Alexandra Mummery
Book Production: John McKercher	Publicity Coordinator: Martha Scarpati
Copy Editor: Susan Lyn McCombs	Rights Coordinator: Diane Gedymin
Indexer: Candace Hyatt	Publisher: Kiran S. Rana

Printed and bound by Bang Printing, Brainerd, Minnesota
Manufactured in the United States of America

9 8 7 6 5 4 3 2 1   First Edition   14 15 16 17 18

Contents

Foreword... *by Pete Carroll, Head Coach of the Seattle Seahawks* . .   ix

Acknowledgments xii

Introduction: Halting the Violence One Bullet at a Time   1
The Reality of Intervention   9

1. The Mindset: Inside Gang Life and Culture   18
Stepping into the Life   19
In the Gang   22
The Culture   26
Law Enforcement   29
Leaving the Gang   31

2. License to Operate: Gaining Street Credibility   33
The Importance of Street Cred   35
How Do You Get It?   38
Maintaining LTO   41
Different Types of LTO   43

3. The Yellow Tape: Managing the Crime Scene   46
First on the Scene   48
Crowd Control   51
Dealing with Law Enforcement   53
Dealing with Paramedics and Firefighters   55

4. The Grapevine: Controlling Rumors   58
Controlling Information Flow   60

Neighborhood Grapevines. 61
Network of Contacts 61
Correcting Wrong Information. 64

5. The White Flag: Negotiating Peace. 66
Fragile Work 68
Mediation. 70

6. The Victims: Dealing with the Grieving. 75
Keeping Emotional Distance 76
Victim Engagement 77
Hospitals 78
Candelight Vigils 80
Funerals 80
Moving Forward. 82

7. Throwdowns and Showdowns. 86
Preparing to Intervene 87
Keeping Cool. 92

**8. Empowering Communities: Restoring
Fractured Neighborhoods**. 98
Community First Responders. 100
Community Intervention and Restoration 101
Community Engagement. 102

9. Baby Mama, Baby Daddy: Handling Domestic Violence 105
Getting Control of the Situation 106
Counseling Jealousy. 109
Changing Attitudes 110

10. Colors on Campus: Understanding the School Dynamic 115
Gang Infiltration. 117
Safe Passage, Safe Houses 120
School Shootings 122
One-on-One Intervention 123

11. Lockup: Adjusting to Life in and out of Prison 126
Back in the Hood 128
The Pen 130
Families 134

12. Street-Savior Syndrome: Surviving the Emotional Toll 135
Dealing with Letdown 136
Setting Limits 137
Finding Family Balance 138
Slipping Back 140
Determining Change 141

**13. Protocols for Peacekeepers: Laying Down Rules
and Regulations** 143
Establishing Rules 144
Protocols for Behavior 145
Procedures and Guidelines 150

14. The Debrief: Reevaluating and Refining 154
Situational Debriefing 155
Frontal Debriefing 156

15. Going Pro: Developing a Corporate Structure 159
Professionalizing 160
Sources of Funding 163
Street Expertise vs. Academic Study 164
National Expansion 165
Global Violence 166

Glossary of Gang Slang 169

Index 171

《 DEDICATION 》

For my beloved mother, who fostered in me the pride and courage to stand up for my beliefs, to always operate with integrity as my foundation, and unflinchingly speak truth in any mission I undertake. For my strong father, who gave me the fortitude to stand my ground with bravery and the resolve to never be cowed by want or fear. For my brother and sister, who lost their existences to the devilish monster of violence, but through their loss, gave me the drive and wherewithal to continue my mission to battle this fiend of violence. For my children, who have forged in me the ability to stay focused, disciplined, energized, and empathetic to carry on this battle so they can live in a better world. For my cherished wife and best friend, who has stood by me, supplied me with constructive support through thick and thin, and never once wavered in lifting me up in good times and bad. For all the true peacekeepers, who have lost their lives in the war against the viciousness of hostility, and for those who have sacrificed their energy, time, and families, and continue to stay true to the mission. They have my highest admiration. Lastly, for all those who have stayed firm with me through this daunting journey. To all of you, I owe the greatest respect and I acknowledge you with a supreme salute.

Foreword

... by Pete Carroll, Head Coach of the Seattle Seahawks

Aquil Basheer has always been a protector and provider unlike anyone else. And not just for the community. For me, too. The first time Aquil and our late friend Bo Taylor took me out on the streets to visit with kids and community members, we stopped at a fried-chicken restaurant to get a late-night snack. While we were choosing our meals, I realized I had left my wallet in the car, so I sneaked out the door as they ordered. Just moments after I had grabbed my wallet from the car in the parking lot and turned to head back into the restaurant, Aquil came running after me, screaming, "What the hell are you doing? You can't do this!"

I was so naïve at that point—what was I thinking just heading out by myself to grab my wallet well past midnight on the streets of L.A.?—but thankfully Aquil was looking after me that night. He had my back then, and he's had it ever since. It's something he does to this day both for me and, more importantly, for our communities as he continues to revolutionize the way youth- and gang-violence issues are resolved and eradicated from our cities. We owe Aquil so much gratitude and appreciation for his passion and dedication to the cause, and for the life-changing and life-saving impact he's had on kids, adults, and communities around Southern California and the world.

I was privileged to meet Aquil more than ten years ago, soon after hearing about kids dying in the streets of L.A. Back in the fall of 2002 the radio on my way to work at USC aired news reports of several children dying in inner-city violence during the previous night. After hearing similar news reports day after day that week, I decided I had to do something to help. The problem struck my heart too deep not to.

Through fortunate circumstances and connections, I was soon introduced to Aquil and his close buddy and cohort Bo Taylor of Unity One. They took me under their wings and taught me all about the issues on the streets and the trage- dies people faced on a daily basis. They took me out at night to meet the players in the communities—kids, parents, leaders, bangers, and everyone in between. Without that connection to Aquil and Bo, I never would've understood the is- sues at play or been involved in helping to find a solution.

Those two men were the initial dominoes that got us started in forming our foundation, A Better LA, in 2003, and they've undoubtedly been indirect but key factors in having the crime rates and homicide stats plummet in Los An- geles during the past decade. Since we started A Better LA, the foundation has celebrated its ten-year anniversary, helped hire dozens of intervention workers, and been a part of incredible change in the city. Additionally, we've started A Better Seattle, which just passed its two-year mark. Aquil remains a vital factor in both foundations and in both cities in immeasurable ways.

Our friend Bo suddenly passed away in 2008, but Aquil has continued to carry on the work to amazing heights. He has a unique mixture of compassion and credibility that sets him apart, whether on the most destitute of streets or in boardrooms of big businesses. His intervention work has not only changed

lives in L.A. but has also become the gold standard for other cities to model. The Professional Community Intervention Training Institute that he leads has an extraordinary ripple effect into communities around the world. He is raising a crew of leaders and influencers who are changing neighborhoods from the inside out. The individuals who give their lives for this work are the MVPs of our communities, and Aquil is the driving force, coach, and patriarch of this tremendously effective model.

Never criticizing or pointing fingers, Aquil has instead decided to proactively approach the issues, create positive change, and save many lives. He is a hero on so many levels.

Our first meeting on the night of my naïve experience outside that fried-chicken restaurant proved to me how much Aquil cared about the safety of all those he knew. It wasn't until later that I realized how much other people truly cared about and respected Aquil. The impact he has had is unprecedented. Aquil's character, discipline, leadership, vision, and ability to connect people have been so impressive, and he has been one of the single most instrumental reasons our communities continue to transform in a positive direction. The intervention workers Aquil trains are the most valuable factors in creating inner-city peace, and we all are so thankful for their work.

But above all, we owe so much appreciation to Aquil for being the spark of change that will flourish for decades to come. And really, after all these words, the most fitting thing we can say is simple: Thank you, Aquil.

PETE CARROLL is head coach of the NFL Seattle Seahawks
and founder of A Better LA and A Better Seattle.

Acknowledgments

There are numerous people and organizations I wish to thank for their support over the years of my work and the Professional Community Intervention Institute. I have tried to center these acknowledgments on the long journey that has resulted in this book, but there are many, many others who deserve to be recognized for their outstanding work. I want to apologize from the start. I know there will be individuals I have neglected to mention here. Please do not take this as a slight. It is not done purposely. If I have missed paying respect to you in these pages, I will get to you sometime in the future.

To my wife, Latifah, who has given me the best thirty-nine years of my life and has been my right arm the entire time, a real soldier who has kept me in check and assisted in bringing out greatness time and again. This work would not have been completed without her patience, resilience, and fortitude. I have been honored and blessed to have her by my side. My children, Lameece, Amir, and Halima, who have been a Godsend, kept me on point, and have stood tall, never complaining about being denied time with me through all my years in the work. They have always understood when I could not be there for them and were never unreasonable in their demands as my children, realizing this was the work their father was put here to do. They have made me proud to be their father. My sister Thelma, a progressive pioneer who uplifted so many with the time she had on the Earth. My brother George, who went through fire and blazed the trail for his siblings to follow. My mother, Naomi, who taught me how to take a stand and what a "real" woman stood for. Her fortitude, inspiration, courage, and throw-down always inspired me to be unstoppable. My father, Van Sr., who taught me how to be a man, to stand up, unbowing, unwavering, uncompromising, and unapologetic. My baby sister, Laura, a true image of a great warrior with the kindest heart in the world. To my brother Van, who was taken by the demon of violence way before his time, of whom I am a reflection, from whom I learned so much. The loss of his life forged me under fire to do this work and was the initial rationale for this book. Cousins Chuck and Sebastian, who have been through hell with me and always have stood tall. Uncles Cecil and Braxton, aunts Connie and Sophia, cousins Charlene and Gene, and a host of other family members who have supported my endeavors.

I owe a tremendous debt of gratitude to my close friends Pete Carroll and Bob Hoff, who have been unwavering in their support of me, my work, and the larger cause of saving besieged communities. I think of both these men more as blood brothers than friends. They have stood by me in the good and bad times, providing advice, guidance, and just damn good friendship. I respect them highly and salute the true integrity, compassion, and caring they have shown me and the thousands of others they have helped. I am honored to have them in my life. I would be remiss if I did not also salute their families, who brought me into their homes as one of theirs. New friend Matt Celenza needs to be saluted for his assistance and unwavering support.

I give my highest thanks to the executive board of A Better LA for believing in our work and staying on point through some very trying times: Bob Best, Nanci Chambers, Lori Forthmann, Sharon Stone, Shane Foley, Pat Haden, Don Kurz, Tim Leiweke, Herb Perlmutter, Joachim Splichal, Antonio Cue, and President Vicente Fox.

I send a much-deserved salutation to ABLA's advisory board, which has provided keen insight, expert direction, and down-home friendship. Ray Bercini, for his special brand of support, brotherhood, and camaraderie; Lynne Rhodes, for her outstanding commitment and personal conversation; Francisco Ortega, for years of camaraderie; Jack Sims, for staying steadfast and providing hope; Scot Obler, for always coming through, ensuring he was there and telling the "correct story"; and Emily Williams, for keeping sanity and balance. A special shoutout for Brother Curtis Woodle, who has been a confidant, warrior, and true brother standing behind me and taking serious blows when few others would. I appreciate our many midnight conversations that kept me from busting down doors and taking numerous individuals to the woodshed!

I would be remiss if I did not acknowledge ABLA's staff members: Rachana Anthony, who has tirelessly stayed on task and true to the mission through all the ups and downs; Jeri Edwards, who has kept me centered and on target; and Kayleigh MacPherson, who is doing an excellent job in documenting the story.

To Julio Marcial and the California Wellness Foundation, for years of superior dedication, support, and close friendship. He has stood above most and has always kept his integrity to the work and people his organization serves. The California Wellness Foundation was one of the first organizations providing the resources to make the PCITI a reality, thanks to his outstanding effort and belief in us.

I wish to thank Celeste Fremon for her exceptional friendship, outstanding vision, and expertise throughout the development of this book. Professor Robert Hernandez, for his savvy, professionalism, and foresight to open this field to his undergrad and grad students and allowing us to be a part of that. Benny Davenport, a "general" in education, a brother who has had my back for over three decades. Jorja and Mark Leap, personal advisors, dear comrades, and close friends who have provided excellent evaluations and recommendations on the work of Maximum Force Enterprises and the PCITI. Jorja has been a confidant, honored friend, and longtime supporter. Dr. Debra Warner, for her vision that teamed up grad students and street professionals to provide the best expertise to besieged communities throughout Los Angeles. She has remained a close business partner and dear friend throughout. Dr. Angie Wolf, one of the most talented and intelligent researchers I know who has been one of my closest allies and advisors, and continues to provide expert analysis. The Los Angeles City and County fire departments and their many members who have been a major part of our work for decades: Chief Kwame Cooper, a close colleague for years, who has worked hand-in-hand with our organization, and Capt. Brent Burton, who has been extremely influential in sharing our expertise with the ranks of emergency responders. Nande Kalenga, city president of the L.A. Stentorians, who has housed us and made sure our needs were met so we could work in our shared training center. The leadership, members, and staff of the L.A. city and county Stentorians, who have backed violence intervention and gone above and beyond to assist us in any way we asked. To the "positive" Los Angeles police and sheriff's department leaders and officers who truly understand and apply community policing strategies and who have been a major component of shifting away from the heavy hand of police suppression. Some key individuals are: LAPD Chief Charlie Beck, former L.A. County Sheriff Lee Baca, Deputy Chief

Bob Green, former Deputy Chief Pat Gannon, Lt. Michael Cardine, and Officer Stinson Brown. A special shoutout to Sgt. Mark Durrell, who got me to view police through a different set of eyes and changed my perception.

Congressman Tony Cardenas, staff member Edward Hewitt, and advisor Mike de la Rocha, who were instrumental in drafting the first definition for the field of community-based gang intervention and designing the "two-prong" approach. Congressmembers Janice Hahn and Bobby Scott, L.A. Mayor Eric Garcetti, L.A. City Councilmen Herb Wesson and Joe Buscaina, and L.A. County Supervisor Mark Ridley-Thomas and his wife, Avis, have all played prominent roles in our success.

The PCITI is only as good as the courageous and dedicated men and women who make up its force of street soldiers. First and foremost, to one of the true pioneers, comrades, and revolutionaries in this work, the late Bo Taylor, one of my closest friends in this work and in life. He deserves to be saluted to the highest degree—he has left an irrefutable mark on this work, and his legacy inspires hundreds to continue the effort to save lives.

To the thousands of certified PCITI Community Intervention First Responder graduates, I salute you for believing in our expertise and staying true to the mission of saving lives and restoring communities. To my inner leadership circle and core PCITI instructors, who have assisted me greatly with their intelligence and expertise in moving forward authentic practitioner-based intervention peacekeeping, you have earned my highest admiration. All of you have done an amazing job in assisting me in developing the PCITI, advancing hard-core intervention and transforming so many who were once a major part of the violence. I consider these focused individuals to be the best in this business who are doing stupendous work as prominent and respected peacekeepers in Los Angeles and throughout the nation.

To the multitudes of "true" peacekeepers, community-based gang-intervention specialists, and community-intervention/crisis-intervention specialists who have done and continue to do this work, who have kept their integrity, stayed true to the work, and formed a major part of peacekeeping efforts. There are too many of you to acknowledge personally, but know that I honor each one of you and your individual efforts to create a healthy environment of peace and wellbeing, to provide a glimmer of hope for both young and old. I truly support you and will always have your back.

To my collaborative partners in Washington, D.C. and Maryland, Penny Griffith and Luis Cardona (and their amazing staff outreach teams), who have joined me in establishing the first and only East Coast/West Coast Regional Gang Intervention Certification Training Program. I celebrate and praise your outstanding efforts to professionalize this work. To our partners in Seattle and Tacoma, Mariko, Eleuthera, Annie, Pam, Greg, Paul, Jova, and the outreach teams in these areas, much respect to all you have done and continue to do. Your efforts set the standard for others to follow.

To James Bolden, for years of documenting, advising, and affording me his ear. He was the first editor to run my first column "Street Survival 101," which allowed me to start telling my story that has culminated in this book. Last but in no way least, to Christina Hoag, who I have much admiration and appreciation for. She has spent grueling hours with me, revising and editing my words and interpreting my thinking process. She has become a very good friend who I respect highly.

AQUIL BASHEER can be reached through his website at
www.maximumforceenterprises.org, by e-mail at takechargeinc@aol.com,
or by calling (800) 926-2155.

INTRODUCTION:
HALTING THE VIOLENCE
ONE BULLET AT A TIME

I had just settled into my armchair at the pad and was looking forward to getting some rest. Big mistake. In the violence-intervention business, this tends to mean exactly the opposite will happen. The pager beeped, instantly shattering my peaceful night. "Need you now, hope you're free," the message read. It gave an address in Southwest Los Angeles. I made some calls to my people on the ground. A mother and daughter had been blasted with a "cannon," a shotgun, in their apartment. It had all the hallmarks of a street assassination. Nope, I wasn't getting any rest. I swooped into my VW Bug with its lowered suspension—fast and small for getting in and out of the hood—and rolled out, arriving about ten minutes later.

It was going to be bad. In the world of gang violence, most victims are young men. That's enough to start a war based on retribution. But killing a woman and child would spark outrage that could easily turn into a bloodbath of revenge. That's where my team and I come in. As professional violence-intervention first responders, our job is to disrupt the endless cycle of payback that turns neighborhoods into yellow-taped crime scenes and to attempt to keep the peace, if at all possible.

I knew the area well. It was plagued with crack houses, pimps and their "strawberries"—the drug-addicted prostitutes who turn tricks for rocks of cocaine—and some of the city's most dangerous "sets"—gangs who battle each

1

other over respect and control of drug turf. Crack cocaine was turning gangsters into millionaires and had turned female bodies into a prime business. Many hard-working families and immigrants were also stuck there, unable to afford housing in safer sections of the city. The escalating drug wars meant I'd been spending a lot of time doing intervention work in the neighborhood in recent months—organizing candlelight vigils for victims, negotiating stand-downs between sets, mediating countless disputes, controlling rampant rumors—in other words, trying to stem the tide of violence, one bullet at a time. When the slaughter of the woman and child occurred, a neighbor of the victims knew to contact me right away. They knew I had street credibility and sincerely cared about the community.

The address was located in an extensive apartment complex of nine cookie-cutter buildings. Police and paramedics had not yet arrived, but a small crowd was milling quietly in the front yard, and the apartment door was ajar. Bad signs. The fact that people were standing at a distance confirmed my suspicion that the carnage inside was devastating.

The woman who had called me pointed silently to the door and shook her head. One of the local homies spoke up. "You might not want to go in there, big bro, it's pretty bad."

"It's cool, soldier, done this many times before," I replied. "Much respect, brother."

"It's on you," he said.

It was essential for me to see exactly what had happened if I was to play any realistic role in halting the predictable cycle of violence that was to come. The neighborhood and the larger community had to have a reliable source of accurate information before the rumor mill took over and the cops clamped down. I steeled the quiver inside me and entered as sirens whooped in the distance.

The Carnage

The living room was dark except for a small, dim light in the corner. I couldn't see anything, but the air felt damp and clammy against my skin. I was hit by a stench I had smelled many times before—straight up death.

As my eyes adjusted, I made out a large mass on the floor. I stepped toward it—a mattress with a lump on top of it. Legs—adult legs. Smaller legs entwined in them. I peered at them—it was a woman hugging a girl, maybe ten years old, obviously trying to shield her from what she must have seen was coming.

I moved closer to see the upper torsos, but I couldn't help but stagger back. The woman's face was gone, as cleanly as if it had been surgically removed with a scalpel. The right side of her skull, her shoulder, and part of her upper arm were missing. She must have turned to protect the girl, her left arm was still around her, but a human body affords scarce protection against a shotgun at close range. The girl's body was shredded like a piece of paper. The force of the blast looked like it had thrown them back three or four feet. They must have been holding onto each other extremely tightly to have remained locked together, or maybe they'd had enough life left in them to embrace each other before expiring.

I have witnessed hundreds of bodies torn by bullets and knives—mangled flesh, pools of blood, spilled organs. You never get used to it—you accept it as a necessary part of the job. But that murder scene was truly horrific, perhaps the worst I have ever seen. Nearly three decades later, I still see it in my mind as clear as if it were yesterday, and it is still a stark reminder of why I do what I do.

The death of children always gets to me. I have three kids, and I always see my own lying there. There is never any excuse for murdering a child. They are the most innocent of victims. This mother and daughter were gunned down brazenly, brutally, and guiltlessly. They had nothing with which to defend themselves. A wave of rage crested inside me.

I had to swallow my emotions to force myself to take another look to make sure I mentally recorded the scene. I knew another look would cause the image to be burned in my mind for the rest of my days, but I had to get what I saw correct if the rumors were to be contained. Blood, tissue, and flesh were splattered all over the walls, the floor, the furniture—that was the source of the strong smell and the dampness. As I walked out of the apartment, I focused on staying clear-minded and rational or I'd be next to useless. Trouble, I knew, was on the way.

It came sooner than I expected. Tires screeched—three cars pulled up, one jumped the curb and came to a halt on the front lawn. The two others stopped diagonally on the street. Three men leapt out, not bothering to close their doors as they raced for the apartment. I knew one of them. I'd seen him in the hood numerous times—he was the victim's brother (although I didn't find that out until later in the day) and was a major player in one of the local sets. He went by the name of Rock and cut an imposing figure, standing over six-feet tall, his body shredded, pure muscle—his biceps as big as my thighs. His bald head gleamed.

"Is she dead?" he hollered, looking in my direction.

I attempted to respond, but the words just wouldn't come out. By his demeanor, I knew the victims must be close to him. My eyes met his, he knew it was bad. He ran on. A few seconds later, a gut-wrenching holler came from the apartment. When he exited, it was clear he did not want consolation.

"Somebody's gonna answer for this! It's payback time! You motherfuckers are gonna die!" he yelled. A blanket of silence smothered the air.

One of my soldiers who had arrived on the scene spoke to one of Rock's people. "Give us some time, brother. We're gonna find out what went down."

"Yeah, homie, get back with us pronto. We gotta move, don't bring no bullshit to the table," he said. That meant we didn't have much time before the cycle of retaliation would start playing out.

Burning rubber, the three men fled seconds before the police pulled up. I left fast, too—I had to start working my contacts on the street to find out what went down before people started shooting whoever they heard was to blame.

But I couldn't start right away. After witnessing these type of scenes, I have to isolate myself for a while to sort through the thicket of emotions that always arise, the multitude of answerless questions. I never cease to wonder about human nature, how some individuals can be so evil and brutally vicious to others. I usually can't eat for a day or so.

Putting in Work

I couldn't afford myself too much time in this case because I knew payback would be swift. Killings generally fall into four categories in the hood—revenge killings for a previous beef, personal killings to intimidate an individual or group, opportunity killings to rob or simply because a convenient victim presented himself, and relationship killings between men and women. None seemed to fit this double slaying, but it wasn't random, either. It appeared very much targeted. But based on my conversations with neighbors, the adult victim didn't have any history of gang or drug involvement, except her brother. Still, it was a stretch to believe his enemies would choose his sister and niece to get to him. He also didn't have a vicious reputation, so it was a long shot that he would merit such a gruesome message, although not impossible.

After several hours, my calls had yielded nothing. The fact that people weren't talking told me this was something big. Usually, sets readily want the word out that they're responsible to shore up their reputation and to instill fear and respect. But nothing was turning over, which meant someone was in hiding, something went wrong, or it was an internal gang beef. I had no choice but to stand down and wait for the grapevine to start filtering back to me. All the while, I knew the clock was ticking—Rock was no chump. He had tight control of the hood and was feared by many. People knew someone was going to pay for this, and soon.

A day or two went by, and the grapevine and my persistent calls turned up something—I found out who *didn't* do it. I was contacted by concerned shot callers, the leaders from the area's two main gangs, who were big drug and turf rivals. Both disavowed responsibility for the killings. They asked what they could do so fingers weren't pointed at them, and requested I set up an informal mediation with each other. I readily agreed. Even if these two gangs weren't responsible for these homicides, it was key to get a ceasefire or stand-down in place, or at least start the process, because one side could start shooting the other over old beefs under the guise of retaliation for this current situation. No leader wants an unnecessary war, or one that his set is not going to benefit from.

I suggested a neutral place outside of either gang's turf—my team's headquarters, which was a private location where we held mediations. Each neighborhood, or set, would send several approved reps whose names had to be vetted by the other side, as well as by my team, in advance. No one wanted hotheads or guys out to make their reputations. No weapons were allowed—everyone had to be patted down before entering.

One of the reps was late so we started the meeting without him. This proved a serious tactical error. We were already in the middle of a heated session when the latecomer came in and sat down at the table. Mad-dogging (staredowns) started going down between the latecomer and a guy in the other hood. It made me uneasy, but the parley was going fairly well so I ignored it.

Suddenly, the latecomer jumped up, pulled out a Smith & Wesson .38 revolver, cocked the trigger, and aimed it in the air. "Fuck all this damn shit!" he yelled. "I'm gonna do what I came here to do!" He flung his chair against the wall.

The atmosphere froze momentarily, although it seemed like an eternity. I stood. In a loud but respectful voice I said, "This ain't the place for that, soldier, this is a place for peace."

One of his homeboys addressed him even more aggressively. "This is not what we're here to do. This is a mediation table, bro, okay? Take that shit out of here! Everybody is here in peace, trying to get to the bottom of this damn thing."

"I don't care about this bullshit!" the guy said. "I'm gonna handle my business."

The set leader again told him it wasn't the venue. The guy shoved the weapon back in his waistband and marched out in a fit of anger. My people followed him to the parking lot to make sure he left.

It was a very tense moment. If he had fired, anything could have happened in that room, and it would have spilled out into the street in a matter of minutes and turned into a full-fledged war in hours. I apologized to the reps from the other gang, who thought they had been set up. The renegade's shot caller also tried to excuse his homeboy's behavior. "That ain't the way we roll," he said. "We handle our business in the street."

The other set didn't buy it at first, but we managed to convince them it wasn't an ambush. Still, it put an end to the mediation right away.

My team's credibility took a hit. I was supposed to guarantee a safe house, but the gun had got through because my security team did not conduct a serious search. They'd rushed it because they wanted to get back to the session. I also had not personally checked out each hood rep because I'd been so busy. After that incident, I implemented stringent security protocols and made sure my staff stuck to them. I also made did my own community background check on each name. It was a valuable lesson I still remember to this day. I made sure this wasn't going to happen again, and it hasn't.

Clarity

I got the warring parties back to the table several weeks later. By then, I had found out what went down with the murders, but I was still trying to confirm the information. The killings were committed by a gang from outside the area that was looking to rob a stash of drugs from the apartment. It turns out they had the wrong address or mistook the apartment since the buildings all looked alike. When the woman said she didn't have anything, they probably thought she was holding out on them and blasted her and her daughter. It was typical of the viciousness of the crack-cocaine wars that were erupting in the neighborhoods.

After finding out that such a callous mistake destroyed two completely innocent lives, I became overprotective of my own family. My wife would have used her body to protect my daughter in the same way that mother had sheltered her child. I immediately called home to check in, firmly instructing my wife and kids to always be on point (careful)—if they were going out, they had to let somebody know where they were going and not go out alone. They shouldn't answer the door if they were not expecting anyone, and always back the car into the garage for a quick getaway.

"We need a survival meeting when I get home," I told my wife.

"What happened?" she said. She knew me well.

After I hung up the phone, I wondered how long I could continue to do this work. But at the same time, I had to continue if I could do anything at all to stop the bloodshed.

Despite the mishap with the first session, the second mediation was as successful as could be expected. The gangs agreed to a sixty-day ceasefire, and we hammered out the terms. They gave each other a "pass," allowing members of each set to walk through the other's neighborhood without being confronted during the risky hours of 7:00 PM to midnight. Women and children were declared off-limits for any actions, and before any street action was taken in payback, reps would be called to clarify the situation before the first bullet was fired. That was a big step forward.

Handling Rock was another fine line we had to walk. I knew he was going to get to somebody. I tried to talk him out of doing further damage, but getting through to him was an uphill battle because the stakes were so high. The killings were a personal affront to him because they involved his family, it was a totally unjustified move, and he had a leadership role that he had to uphold—the hood was expecting retaliation and he had to maintain their respect. "Brother," he would say to me after one of our talks, "I got respect and love for you, but this ain't the time. We both know I got to answer this for my hood, but, more importantly, for myself."

It was obvious he wasn't going to listen to me. I had to find another way to reach him. I enlisted the aid of his homeboys, emphasizing to them that if he took action and got popped (arrested), there would be extreme legal consequences because of his jacket, his criminal history. He could go down for a long, long stretch. The homies could see the reasoning behind that, but they also knew the code of the streets dictated a response—a huge one. They also knew it didn't have to happen at that moment. Everybody was waiting for a response from Rock, including law enforcement. His crew reasoned they needed to convince Rock of that. His people hustled him out of Los Angeles for an extended period, so he could distance himself and cool down.

Community Mobilization

My work still wasn't done. The community was becoming riled up at law enforcement's lack of progress in solving this case and many other homicides, as well as the general lack of public safety. The community felt the police had abandoned them. Children couldn't walk to school without being accosted by dope dealers. Prostitutes openly solicited customers in broad daylight. Warring sets armed with AK-47s controlled street corners and parks, leaving kids with no place to play and making even walking to the corner store a risk for anyone.

A town hall meeting was called. More than a hundred and fifty people packed a community center to vent their frustration to police and city leaders, who made vague promises of stepped-up patrols and youth programs.

But many in the community felt they were being paid no more than lip service, and if they wanted action, they'd have to do it themselves. I was asked by community leaders to conduct community survival trainings that taught residents how to spot signs of an imminent breakout of violence on the street and how to set up citizen patrols, among other things. Schools requested my after-school youth development and empowerment program that instilled moral values. The community was taking action, without help from law enforcement or the city.

The ceasefire held, but soon any other suspicious death that occurred in that area was being attributed to revenge for the mother–daughter murder. People took advantage of the high emotions around those killings to avenge themselves on old rivals or spark new feuds in the name of payback. Over the next six months I looked into eight killings that the grapevine linked to the mother–daughter murders, but they all turned out to be down to other causes. On each one I had to do fact-checking with my contacts on the street to find out the real lowdown so a new cycle of violence would be avoided.

A woman killed in her car in a fast-food drive-through line as her children watched, turned out to be a domestic-violence case that had spun out of control. A triple murder on a front porch by a shooter who walked up to them and fired was part of an unrelated gang war. A seven-year-old girl slain as she played with dolls in her front yard was the mistaken target for two sixteen-year-olds who were at the back of the house. All were originally linked to the slaying of Rock's sister and niece.

Three other deaths did prove to be remotely related to that killing. A home invasion claimed two lives, one of them being a close relative of the murdered mother. I found out through street contacts that the mother's money and valuables were rumored to be stored at this relative's home, motivating the home invasion. Another close relative of the mother committed suicide after a police standoff, having become mentally unstable after the mother's killing.

For eight months my team and I worked on interventions related to the mother–daughter murders, which the police never solved, as well as numerous other interventions that cropped up. Our efforts paid off, and the street simmered down considerably. If we, and a few other key groups, had not been there, I hate to think how far the spiral of violence could have reached.

» The Reality of Intervention

This is the unseen work of professional hard-core street intervention—it takes a lot of guts but rarely, if ever, brings any glory. Results are often measured in what *didn't* happen, not what did. That's the goal of violence intervention—to stop the bloodshed on our streets in a way that law enforcement and others can't. We stop it from the inside, not the outside.

Intervention and prevention are major tools of the fight against violence. They don't replace some of the traditional measures: social services, schools, parenting, law enforcement, and personal development, which are all essential pieces of the equation. Instead, intervention and prevention work equally alongside those elements and bring expertise and authority that other agencies lack—we have been there, we have lived the violence. In my view, we need all the tools and skills we can lay our hands on if we are to combat the epidemic of violence in our society.

My mission is a holistic one—to repair broken communities, stop bloodshed, and attempt to provide hope to the many individuals who have lost faith. I am a hard-core community-violence gang interventionist. Some of the worst violence I deal with relates specifically to gangs. They are a big part of the reason why our communities need repair. Crime and violence petrifies a community, locks it into despair and fear, robbing it of progress and hope.

Gangs are a scourge no one has been able to solve or even make a dent in. Instead the opposite has happened. They have spread across the United States and the world. In Los Angeles and other big cities such as New York and Chicago, gangs have been deeply entrenched for decades. In Los Angeles County, the nation's unofficial gang capital, gang population estimates range from 700 to 1,100 street gangs with 50,000 to more than 100,000 members. No one really has an accurate headcount. What police do know is that 80 percent of crime in Los Angeles, ranging from home invasions to homicide, is rooted in gang-related causes.

Police have also come to realize they cannot combat the gang epidemic alone. As Los Angeles Police Chief Charlie Beck often says, "we cannot arrest our way out of this." Law enforcement has seen time and again that as soon as one set is taken down, more shot callers and soldiers pop up to take the place of those behind bars. Poverty, lack of jobs, and low-quality schools create a never-ending supply of candidates who don't see opportunity anywhere else.

Once gangs take hold in a neighborhood, the community changes dramatically. Young men are challenged if they walk down an unfamiliar block, fifth-graders are recruited to sell drugs on their way to school, parks become gang hangouts instead of children's play areas, businesses are forced to pay protection money, people have to be careful about what color clothing they wear in a particular neighborhood—the wrong color shirt or cap in the wrong place can bring a hail of gunfire.

Gangs are no longer just a big-city phenomenon. They are extending their influence as they seek new markets for their drug trade and other criminal businesses, including human trafficking, prostitution, and robberies. In the last couple years, I've been called to train interventionists and set up mediation programs in Little Rock, Arkansas; Atlanta, Georgia; Corpus Christi, Texas; Seattle and Tacoma, Washington; and Omaha, Nebraska, places I never expected to have gang issues. We have also worked in cities with longstanding gang problems: New York; Chicago; Oakland, California; and Washington D.C.

The reach of my team has also extended internationally. We have been called in to do trainings and help develop the public safety infrastructure in Ghana, Egypt, Argentina, Brazil, Peru, El Salvador, Canada, and China, to name a few.

With adjustments to the needs of each community, intervention can be adapted to rural areas, small and large cities, and to any culture because the premise is simple: Violence and those who practice it have common denominators, so we have developed operational procedures and responses to deal with it. We come from the communities where hostility and violence are part of everyday life, so we know what it's like to live with it. We don't judge people, because we've been there. People can talk to us because they know our role is not to arrest them or turn them in, take their children away, or kick them out of school. We don't carry weapons. The only authority we have comes from the community itself—our street credibility, what we call an "LTO," a license to operate. The LTO is the basis of how we work.

Forged from the Culture

The majority of interventionists are former gang members and community activists—I was forged in the culture as a respected militant and enforcer in the Black Power movement in the late sixties and early seventies. That background assisted me well when I joined the Los Angeles Fire Department in 1980. I worked for thirty-two years as a firefighter, mostly as a specialized fire inspector. Besides gangs, interventionists also deal with situations involving generalized street violence, domestic violence, at-risk youth and school safety, community mobilization, and felon rehabilitation and re-integration into society. We work with both the victims and the perpetrators in communities where standard solutions have not met with much success.

Hard-core intervention work is not for everyone. Stepping into the unforgiving world of violence and mayhem is stressful, challenging, and takes a toll on you and your family. It involves a delicate balancing act. Interventionists cannot get involved in the vices of gang life, but we have to remain close enough to the gang environment to maintain ties and influence, and gather the street intelligence we need to operate. We must work to steer youth away from gangs but cannot judge gang lifestyle. We are not police informants but must maintain a loose working relationship with right-minded, community-based law enforcement and other public-safety agencies.

The work can be physically dangerous, mentally taxing, and downright disheartening at times. We are dealing with people who see violence as a source of their self-esteem, a badge of honor, and a normal way of doing business. For some, it's a family tradition going back as many as three generations. In a shoot-first-ask-questions-later climate, a wrong word, look, or gesture, or even just the perception of such, can result in immediate gunfire. Getting in the middle of this mindset requires highly developed interpersonal skills; cool, rational thinking; and a lot of commitment. I emphasize the latter. Many interventionists start with good intentions, but a large percentage fall by the wayside, unable to cope with the emotional challenges, the lack of resources, and the low level of appreciation for the work. A few are unable to resist re-entering gang life. The reward for doing this work is largely found in the form of a teary-eyed hug from a mother, father, sister, or brother at 1:00 AM, and from within—knowing you helped save a life, a family, and possibly a community.

Coming from this culture and putting in over four decades of experience on streets all over this country and others, I have learned what to do and what not to do. I now train hundreds of former gang members and many types of professionals, including graduate students and public-safety experts, to be certified peacekeepers in an eighteen-week course, which includes a four-week internship practicing on the streets what they learned in the classroom.

Professionalizing the Work

The Professional Community Intervention Training Institute (PCITI) has been endorsed by the Los Angeles City Council as an official City of Los Angeles community-based gang-interventionist training course and has been validated by experts at the University of California-Los Angeles, the University of Southern California, The Chicago School of Professional Psychology, the Los Angeles police and fire departments, and numerous others.

The PCITI has since become a national model for gang-intervention/violence-abatement practitioner-based training. In Seattle, the Seattle Seahawks NFL team contracted us to work with the Seattle Youth Violence Initiative and the Alive & Free program to professionalize and certify gang-interventionist outreach workers in that city. In neighboring Tacoma, we partnered with the Northwest Leadership Foundation to train outreach intervention specialists and organize a certified gang outreach team.

The U.S. Department of Justice's Division of Juvenile Justice and Delinquency Prevention funded a gang-intervention program we set up with partner organizations in Maryland. Public and private agencies in Delaware and the District of Columbia have also tapped us to launch intervention initiatives and develop the nation's only unified regional community-violence and gang-intervention certification training course.

Working on the other side of the fence, we have trained numerous firefighters, paramedics, law-enforcement officers, mental-health professionals, parks and recreation workers, school teachers, anti-domestic-violence advocates, and social-service workers in Atlanta, Arkansas, Texas, and numerous California cities about how to deal with gangs, youth hostility, and community violence.

PCITI instructs participants in our standard operating procedures and protocols that cover topics such as targeted communication with people on the street, controlling emotional crowds at crime scenes, quashing rumors that lead to retaliatory shootings, talking people out of brandishing guns and knives, negotiating gang truces and ceasefires, setting up candlelight vigils, consoling grieving relatives, and mediating turf conflicts, just to name a few key topics. We get different points of view from guest lecturers including social-service experts, mental-health specialists, law-enforcement officers, prosecutors, emergency responders, and probation officers. We also teach crisis first aid, CPR, and electronic-paddle use, and students become certified in these areas.

The process of personal development, psychological transformation, and individual refinement is another big part of our work. Attempting to change the destructive mindset and acceptance of using violence and replacing it with socially constructive alternatives is an extremely important task we do as interventionists. Many of our students have had little formal education, have spent years in prison, and have had little exposure to life beyond their neighborhood. Through exercises I designed with psychology professors and other specialists, students are taught to overcome racist and sexist attitudes, gang rivalries, feelings of low self-worth, hostility to law-enforcement and fire personnel, negative cultural stereotypes, and much more.

In addition to the comprehensive instruction on operational street protocol, former gang members learn respect for themselves and others, how to dress and conduct themselves professionally, specialized speaking skills, ethical standards of behavior, and how to develop organizational standards. They also learn about accountability and atonement, and to obtain self-respect based on productive actions rather than destructive actions. Other professionals who take the course learn firsthand about the dynamics and intricacies of gang life and its associated violence, as well as the role of interventionists and how we work. Thus, they gain a much deeper understanding of gang culture, equipping them to provide better assistance to those in "the life."

Getting to this point has been a long journey. For years, a handful of interventionists including myself were working the streets on our own. Many police officers rejected us as interfering with their jobs, while others thought we were shams, using a do-gooder guise to hide gang activity. The establishment refused to believe that underprivileged people from the inner-city could be something other than a destructive force, that we could be a force for positive change in our own community.

It wasn't until the 1992 civil disturbance in Los Angeles after the acquittal of the police officers who beat Rodney King that civic leaders sought us out to help heal a fractured community. Even then it was a battle, but the need for solutions prevailed over initial cynicism. Since then, we have slowly gained recognition for our work, and now officials across the nation reach out to us for help as a matter of course.

When an interventionist was shot to death by a graffiti tagger, the Los Angeles Mayor's Office asked interventionists to spread the word with gangs that it was not a gang-related killing in order to avert a revenge shooting. When the grand-parents of a child killed in gang crossfire could not cross the border from Mexico to attend their grandson's funeral, interventionists called a congressman's office. The grandparents got through. When in the summer of 2011 South Los Angeles saw a spike in gang shootings, police requested more interventionists on the ground to help tamp down the violence that threatened to spiral out of control.

In 2010, as I stood up at a ceremony to receive the California Peace Prize from the California Wellness Foundation, the highlight of a year of awards given to my organization and me for our long-term work against violence, my mind cast back to the first time I realized the pivotal role intervention can play in saving lives.

MUHAMMAD

I was hanging out one afternoon with some friends in the front of the pool table shop owned by several of my uncles and my grandfather, which was a gathering place back in the heyday of the Black Power movement in the late sixties and early seventies in Los Angeles. A homie burst through the door.

"They shot Muhammad!"

"Who shot him?"

"The police! They killed him!"

We didn't waste any time. We sprinted down Broadway, stopping cold when we saw the mound covered with a red-stained white sheet, lying on the ground next to a small Datsun.

Muhammad was a friend of mine, about ten years older than me, who I had met through an uncle, Big C. He had been a street hustler, selling a little dope here, doing a little pimping there. But then he became an orthodox Muslim. With that robe and kufi (skullcap), he turned his life around. He got a job with the city transit department and took care of his wife and four kids. He became well liked and respected in the neighborhood.

A crowd had gathered around the body. It was getting bigger and anger was rising. People started hollering at the cops.

"Why'd you shoot him?" "He wasn't doing anything, why'd you shoot him?" "Why'd you have to kill him?"

(cont'd.)

The story emerged. Muhammad had been pulled over by cops for a reason that was unclear, and they asked him to get out of the car, which was standard procedure back then. He complied, and gave them his license. Then they demanded that he lie face down on the ground, another standard operating procedure aimed at humiliating and intimidating blacks and Latinos at that time.

Muhammad refused since he was all dressed up—he was driving home from a wedding. There was some arguing back and forth, then he got back in his car. The cops pumped him full of lead. They claimed it was a justified homicide.

A lot of people had witnessed the whole scene and they were fuming. Pressure had been building in the community for a long time. People were fed up with harassment and abuse by the nearly all-white police force. Black people got stopped and hassled for no reason, arrested on trumped up charges, beaten down and had guns pointed at them. Muhammad's death was the last straw.

Over the next few days, there was talk of storming the 77th Street police station, people yelled "pigs!" at cops in the street, lobbed rocks and bottles, and even shot at squad cars. In response, the police cracked down, determined to make an example of the troublemakers. Tensions were rising to a fever pitch. I could see both sides appeared to be on track to a full-scale, head-on collision that wouldn't benefit anybody.

With my cadre from my martial arts school and using all the street credibility I had, I started organizing meetings with the main groups in the area—the Nation of Islam and other Muslim groups, the brothers from the Malcolm X Center, the black nationalists, and street gangs—to get them to stand down. I wanted them to at least back off as the case wound through the police department administrative procedures. It had nothing to do with being pro-police, it had everything to do with attempting to stop a lot of brothers from being killed. It wasn't easy. These groups were hell-bent on revenge and didn't like anyone telling them to stop agitating. I kept repeating that the cycle had to be broken or the violence would get worse. They pulled back.

I also met several times with police brass at the 77th Street station, who were particularly hostile. I attempted to explain why the community was so riled up and said we wanted better, more-respectful treatment from the police. A few key commanders eventually understood, but a lot of the officers in the field did not.

We managed to defuse a lot of heated tempers. The police officers who killed Muhammad were later exonerated, which brought about another wave of hostility, but Muhammad's family received a wrongful death settlement from the city. That served to calm tensions considerably.

That was one of my first community interventions. I saw it could be accomplished. It just took someone to step up and do the work. Over the following four decades, that's what I have done. My co-author Christina Hoag and I have now written this book to share my knowledge and experience. It is our aim for the book to serve as an instructional tool for intervention workers, public-safety professionals, and municipal governments, as well as average citizens seeking ways to stop the violence that preys upon our communities. This book can serve as a manual for anyone who deals with the different types of violence in the course of daily life, whether on the streets, in schools, or even in prison. *Peace in the Hood* is another step in my life's mission to end the violence.

Authors' note: The anecdotes in the book are all true, but names have been changed to protect people from potential incrimination or embarrassment.

1 THE MINDSET: INSIDE GANG LIFE AND CULTURE

Tony had recently got out of the pen and was doing major damage on the streets—robbing, shooting, fronting dealers who were slinging. He and his people were disrupting long-held peace treaties with a total lack of respect. The hoods were getting pissed off, and a major truce was in danger of going up in smoke. I had known the young brother for years. He was a good dude: small but buff, physically tough. He had trained in my martial arts academy, the Association of Unified Street Fighters, when he was a teenager. An associate called me to see if I could somehow rein him in.

"Big Homie, your boy's about to set off a war. Word is if somebody don't contain that fool, he and some of his people gonna end up in boxes."

I set up a sit-down with Tony in the back room of a bakery one night. As I drove over there, I got to thinking about the brother's past, wondering if I could have done more to keep him from the life, if I should have put in more time with him.

Tony was seventeen when he found his pops dead on the couch one night. His father had become a chronic alcoholic after his wife left the family. Tony and his fourteen-year-old sister survived on their father's general relief check in a tiny house in the backyard of a larger house in South L.A. But after his pops died and the meager welfare check along with him, Tony had to find a way to take care of himself and his sister to avoid becoming wards of the state.

I mentored him on numerous aspects of life, tried to prepare him for work and get him a job, gave him money when he needed it. But he was soon months behind on the rent. He found a solution—the local hood—and started pulling burglaries and assaults on pimps, dope pushers, and local businesses. Without any proper female guidance, his sister turned to prostitution and drugs. There was nothing I could do or say to get him out of the life. As he got deeper into it, I had to put some space between us because I was trying to create peace in the hood and Tony wasn't about that.

When I met Tony at the bakery, he was thin and jumpy, packing firepower, and likely strung out. It had been years since I had seen him. He didn't seem at all concerned when I told him threats were surfacing against him. "The word is you need to lay low, get off the streets for a minute. I agree with what's being said, sounds like you really need to go underground," I said.

"We just handling our business, responding to what been brought to us," he said.

"Seems like a lot of hoods don't like your way of handling business," I replied.

The meeting was brief. It ended with the street sign of brotherhood, a clasped handshake followed by bumping the chest twice with the fist, and with me wondering if the message got through to him.

It seemed to. Things calmed down and the soldiers on the street were appeased, but Tony had made a lot of enemies. About a month later, a rival set confronted him and some of his homies. A shootout erupted—two of Tony's soldiers got wasted (killed), and another was wounded. One of the rivals was also iced. Tony disappeared.

❯❯ Stepping into the Life

Youngsters join gangs for a variety of reasons. For Tony, the life gave him economic survival, a structure that replaced the family that disintegrated on him, and an outlet for rage. One of the most basic reasons kids join gangs is to get their needs fulfilled. It can be a psychological need: a sense of belonging, for structure and rules, for life purpose and direction, for recognition and respect. It can be a material need: for protection from other gangs or bullies, for financial wherewithal. It can also be a family tradition, sometimes going back three generations, an expectation to be fulfilled. For some impressionable young adolescents, it's simply the glamour of the "gangsta" lifestyle—the cars, the ladies, the power, the paper (money), the glitters and the bling—that attracts them.

Most gang members join between the ages of twelve and fifteen, usually after spending time hanging around the fringes of a set. It is imperative to understand the lure to understand the culture. In some cases, gang membership is the first time youngsters have felt any real self-esteem and power in their lives.

The words of a twenty-two-year-old set member nicknamed Little Cane, because he carried a cane to serve the double purpose of style and a weapon, have always stayed with me. "Big Homie," he told me, "I love this life, I'm gonna live this lifestyle till I die. Up until I got with the set, I didn't know what living was all about. I was always having to ask for money, people didn't take me serious. I had to beg, borrow, or steal for everything. I tried to do it the so-called right way, but all that got me was being punked, abused, and misused. But people ain't gonna be saying 'Little Cane' no more. They gonna be saying 'Big Cane.'" That's a deal that's hard to counter.

Sometimes it just seems to be what all their peers are doing. "It's hard for a teenager not to end up in a gang," said former gang member Juan, who was convicted of gang-related crimes and deported to his native Honduras where he left the life. "All your friends are in it, your older brothers. It's something you have to do, but it's also something you want to do."

The solidarity of a brotherhood especially appeals to kids who come from broken or dysfunctional homes where they never felt supported. "It's like belonging to a family—'I'll give my life for my homie and he'll give his for me'," Juan said.

Across different cities, cultures, and countries, poverty is the widespread common denominator among gangs. The reason why communities are besieged by violence most often comes down to deprivation. Poverty breeds the sense of despair and anger that life offers few, if any, options. You don't see the same number of gangs in middle-class suburbs where kids see the future as holding possibilities. Nor do all inner-city youth join gangs. In fact, most don't. But for the ones who do, it's because they just don't see anything else on the horizon. Set membership is something that's within their reach. It's easily attainable and yields immediate results.

HOLLOWPOINT

Hollowpoint got his nickname because he packed a 9mm with a ten-shot clip loaded with illegal bullets, and he didn't hesitate to use them—he was a shooter. I was breaking bread with Point one evening, and we got to talking about his life. "Where you going from here, young brother? What you gonna do when you get to my age? What about family, children, a wife?" I asked him.

"Man, I ain't gonna never have that type of life. That ain't for me. I done put too many rivals in the ground. I know when my time come I'm gonna be blasting."

"Naw, Point, you ain't got to go out like that," I said. "There's ways out of the life. A lot of us have done it, but it ain't easy, it doesn't come without bruises."

"Brother Aquil, when you and your people were out there, that was a different time. All I can hope for is to be idolized, have my name remembered for standing up and not punking out for anyone or anything. In all honesty, that's the way I want it. I get everything I want out of this life—bitches, dope, money, rep. Man, there ain't no more to life than that."

Gang members accept that the good times might not last long. For those seriously in the life, prison or death seems a fair tradeoff for that short, intense burst of getting what they want.

Once in the gang culture, life becomes literally do or die. Members don't have time to think about the consequences, either for themselves or anyone else. To them, their choices are justified because they've felt betrayed since birth. Parents abandon them, schools are apathetic, neighborhoods have no jobs, racism and prejudice provide limited opportunities. The feeling of having the right to balance the scales because society has done you wrong is a given. Living fast and hard becomes an accepted norm. The culture justifies leading angry, accelerated lives because you figure you'll be dead by the age of twenty anyway. Going down in a time-honored blaze of bullets is a way of making your life matter because you don't perceive that anything else will do that. Gang membership is a way of ensuring you put some sort of honor in your life, even if it leads to death or prison.

Little Cane summed it up: "Moms keeps talking about how I'm gonna die if I don't change my ways. Something gonna happen to me and she gonna be minus a son. Hell, we all gonna die sometime, and I want to go out in an inferno, everybody gonna know. All I can tell you, this is me. I ain't changing. This is my life, and I'm gonna live it full blast."

》In the Gang

New members are initiated into the gang in many ways. Sometimes there's a "jump-in," a beating for a short period of time where the candidate must absorb the blows and kicks to show his toughness, or he might have to "put in work," do some damage on the street to someone. Each set has its own initiation rite. After you're in, you are expected to live by a set of rules, a code of honor, and to put in the work that's required of you. The way members move up in the hierarchy is by putting in that work—blasting rivals and anyone else who doesn't meet the set's approval, slinging drugs, repeatedly showing loyalty to the gang's mission by following orders without question and living by the code.

Gangs form in a variety of ways, mostly along racial and ethnic lines, although there are now Latino members of traditionally black gangs in neighborhoods where Latinos have moved in. Each racial subset of gangs shares loose, general characteristics, although there are many differences within that subset. Generally speaking, Latino gangs tend to be low profile, very closely knit, almost family-like, and tightly structured with a strict hierarchy. Black gangs are more geographically oriented and money driven. Asian gangs are noted for their ruthlessness and usually operate with a more underground culture. They also tend to be very insular, moving among and preying mostly on their own community, thereby escaping a lot of public attention. White gangs are more race oriented, although of late they have adopted many traits of their ethnic rivals, and some are even aligning themselves with them to a certain degree.

Although each specific set has its own rules, gangs share some general ones, including not killing children or elderly people, targeting gang members' families, or snitching to law enforcement. Some rules have weakened in recent years because many younger gang members are not following the traditional code and are establishing their own structures and operating protocols. They are more ruthless and eager to show their power and instill fear. What used to be strictly off the table is no longer that way, with the exception of snitching and a few other components.

Tattoos and colors are two of the main ways gangs identify themselves. Black gangs have traditionally used more colors—the two most notorious ones being red representing the Bloods and blue representing the Crips. But the use of colors, such as a cap, shirt, or a bandana in the back pocket, is not as widespread as it used to be because it signals "gang member" to law enforcement.

Most gangs, regardless of ethnicity, now use more tattoos and other signets. But colors are still used loosely, and wearing the wrong color in the wrong neighborhood is a cause to move on individuals with either threats or bullets. People, especially men, in gang-turf neighborhoods must avoid wearing the local set's colors, its preferred style of clothes, even the brand. Latino and Asian gangs, to a certain degree, rely more on heavy tattooing to denote affiliations.

Gang tattoos are most often in black ink, not colored, although there are always exceptions. Tats can depict not only a member's gang affiliation but also his history within the gang—the shootings and killings he's been involved in, his status in the set, and so on. This is also true for prison gangs. Some common gang tats include teardrops at the corner of an eye or the Greek masks of tragedy and comedy signifying the gang philosophy of "smile now, cry later," that the present is all that matters.

Tattoos also carry another meaning to gangs—they are etched into a person's skin, representing the depth of gang loyalty, the pride and permanence in membership. The decision to get gang tattoos removed is a huge one, meaning a complete break with the life.

Gang Hierarchies

At the top of the gang hierarchy are the O.G.s—original gangsters—the elders, the veterans who have survived. These are diehard members who are proud of their gang affiliation and will carry it throughout their lives. Oftentimes, they'll semiretire from actively participating in gang affairs, but their word still carries extreme weight. They're allowed to do that because they've paid their dues. But they still demand and enjoy the respect they get from being an O.G. affiliated with a particular set and the work they put in.

The royalty of the neighborhood are the "double O.G.s" and "triple O.G.s," meaning their affiliation goes back two or three generations. L.A. is now in the third generation of gang warfare, and gang affiliation has become a proud family tradition in many neighborhoods. People brag about their familial relationship to a founder of a particular set or a particularly notorious gangster. That gives them status in the community.

Shot callers are the set leaders. They run the show, commanding the soldiers in the street, the regular members. Oftentimes, they're more charismatic individuals that people seem to naturally flock to, and they have been tested and have proven themselves both mentally and physically in the streets. They also may simply be the more ruthless, manipulative soldiers that people fear more. They back up their word at all costs—their throwdown is legendary.

Enforcers and shooters carry out the hard-core work of the gang. Affiliates, associates, and crews make up the bulk of gang membership. Here you get a range of people. Some are dabblers, participating in just enough gang activity so they can reap some of the benefits of membership—girls, fast money, status. Some are sociopaths who are in it because they enjoy the violence and mayhem.

At the bottom of the list are the hangers on—the young wannabes and the groupies. The wannabes are frequently the most dangerous because they need to earn gang members' respect to be admitted into the gang. They'll do whatever needs to be done, and gang members know it. They tend to be young, with clean rap sheets, so if they get caught in a robbery, burglary, or shooting, their punishment will be slight, leaving them available for other deeds.

The groupies like the parties and the drugs. They look to gain status by simply hanging out with those who have it. This includes a lot of the gang girlfriends.

Gang Turfs

Gangs tend to operate in very small worlds. In Los Angeles, no one lives more than a few miles from the Pacific Ocean, yet many children grow up without ever seeing it. They may never see the other side of the city where white people live. They may never walk into the mountains that surround the city. They don't know much more than their own neighborhood, maybe because their families don't have a car and so they're limited to bus routes. Gang membership tends to reinforce those small worlds. Gang members often lose or must alter their status when they move in other spheres. In the neighborhood they're somebody with real rep; outside it, they are usually not.

To a gang member, the word "neighborhood," "hood," or in Spanish, "barrio," refers to a physical geographical area in which a "set" or "click" (also "clique," or "clica" in Spanish), a gang subset, resides. So they stick close to home to maintain their self-esteem. That helps keep their vision tunneled and maintains the unique, many would say negative, value system. It also helps them keep control of their turf. The geographic area they reign over may be small, but the control can be substantial, deciding who can walk down the street or who sells items on the sidewalk, for instance. That control bolsters their sense of power and forces respect, or at least assent, from the community.

I should note here that a new level of gang has developed in recent years. Sets have expanded their reach beyond their hoods as they seek markets without a lot of competition to push their products. Law-enforcement efforts such as gang injunctions, which prohibit gang members from congregating in public, and large-scale takedowns are other major reasons gangs have sought new ground. Now you can find branches of gangs using the name of their original neighborhood in new cities—the Grape Street Crips from Los Angeles in New Jersey, for example.

Graffiti is an important way for gangs to control their turf. "Tags," which often look like jumbles of chicken scratch in black ink, but which are actually a system of writing unto themselves, serve as the gang's newspaper. To those who know how to read them, the markings tell what's going on in the turf—who's beefing with who, who's warring, who's got a hit on them, the latest gang exploit. Tags have also become a way to measure a community's response to a gang.

If the tags are left up for more than forty-eight hours, the community has been beaten down by the gang and lives in fear of it. If the tags are whitewashed right away, the community has mobilized to some degree and is actively trying to limit gang activities. Painting out tags is an important statement by the community affected by gang life, but it cannot be undertaken lightly as it will usually spark a response from the gang.

Becoming Hardened

All gang members become hardened by the life to some degree. The longer a member is in the life, the more hardened he becomes, the more depersonalized. As in combat, depersonalization is an essential part of surviving in the gang mindset. Members can shoot, maim, and kill in cold blood because they don't see their victims as "victims." To them, victims are not human beings who are sons, fathers, brothers. They don't see the pain of a child growing up fatherless. They don't see the eternal grief of a parent losing a child. To them, there's no tragedy in a life ended before it's even been lived.

Similar to combat soldiers, the victims are depersonalized into faceless enemies who will kill me if I don't kill them first. There is no remorse. They don't lack empathy, but because they've mentally depersonalized the enemy into a subspecies of human that is not worthy of empathy, they can kill them.

There is hell to pay, however, when the opposing gang kills one of the homeboy's own. Then they feel and see the pain. Since gang members may have gone through literal life and death situations together, shared intense emotional experiences involving danger and fear, or shared similar dysfunctional family problems, the bonds among them can be strong. When one of their own is lost, the mourning is intense.

I've often been asked why gang members don't see the senselessness in killing each other over a graffiti tag scrawled on a wall on someone's block or someone walking through a neighborhood controlled by another gang. How can they not see that those things aren't worth taking a life? The answer is because those turf rules are their belief systems, their source of self-worth. All of us operate from a system of values and beliefs that defines what we do and what we stand for. The gang belief system just happens to be different from the one dictated by society.

» The Culture

I always like to say gang culture revolves around the "7 R's"—**respect, revenge, retaliation, retribution, review, revisit, revenue.**

Respect and disrespect define everything in the life. How one determines that respect depends on the circumstances and environment one has been raised in. This is why it's very hard to understand the mentality if you have never been in or around the life. This is not a justification of gang culture by any means. It's just a reality that has to be comprehended. When gang members perceive disrespect, it is an attack on their core. It is human nature that when we feel deeply attacked, we attack back. Attacking back to correct a perceived lack of respect is the very essence of gang psychology.

Getting respect from others is a reason why many youngsters join gangs in the first place. They never got respect from their families, or earned good grades that would've won them respect at school. So they get respect by belonging to

an organization that makes itself respected by sowing fear or acquiring a degree of wealth way out of proportion to what others their age make. They and their families often don't have any tools like a diploma or a degree, a career or a good job, a nice house and car, that would get them respect in the world. In the world of the street, the way you gain respect is your reputation, your word, your throw-down. You're judged on whether you keep it. That's it.

Gaining respect was a big reason Juan joined a gang. He saw his parents, immigrants from Honduras, working in McDonalds and picking aluminum cans out of the trash to sell for recycling. "I was ashamed of my father. I made fun of him for working those jobs, and I said I wasn't going to be like that," he said. Gangs, on the other hand, had money, girls—and respect. "They became my role model."

When there's any kind of slight to your reputation, even a perceived one, it has to be taken as an affront because the more you respond to disrespect, the more respect you earn. That often includes violence because then the person who's doing the dissing—and others—will respect you out of fear, if nothing else.

That leads right into an endless cycle of **revenge, retaliation,** and **retribution.** Each side seeks to regain its respect after being disrespected by the other. Violence is the commonly chosen method because it leaves the most fear and makes the biggest statement. That's what gang warfare is all about.

After the violent act, the set will **review** and **revisit** what happened, improving the operation and getting ready for the inevitable next round of violence.

Members from the culture train hard. They study their adversaries for opportunities of weakness when they can strike, devise offensive plans of action, prepare defensive counterstrikes.

That leaves **revenue.** A lot of gang beefs revolve around money and getting more of it. That's a key aspect of gang life because of the lack of opportunity for inner-city youth. Jobs are few and far between in the neighborhoods, local schools are inferior and inadequately prepare youngsters for the labor market. But people still want material goods, the same as everybody else. The gang offers ways to be able to afford them.

It's a gigantic myth, however, that gang members are intellectually inferior. They may not be highly educated, but there's nothing wrong with their intellect, some without doubt have high IQs and could have succeeded in professional careers if they'd made other life choices and were given a chance. Overall, they are street savvy.

They usually are not naturally violent. But the culture changes their thinking process and instills a set of values and priorities that could be called antisocial, which is needed to survive in their chosen lifestyle. A member is pushed to do things he normally wouldn't do, namely the predatory skills of shooting, robbing, and drug dealing, to define his prowess to the extreme. The more brazen, the more wanton the act, the higher the member's prestige.

Only about 10 to 15 percent of gang members are the real hard-core, ruthless types who are into violence for the sake of violence. They like the power that instilling fear in others gives them. This fulfills a need in them driven by an inner powerlessness caused, for example, by growing up in homes where abuse was rampant and the child could not fight back or was unprotected. These are often the toughest members to reach.

PIGTAIL

Pigtail got her name from her hairstyle—she combed her hair into two balls on the side of her head, kind of like Mickey Mouse ears. She was a small fifteen-year-old who made up for her lack of height with a firecracker personality, responding to people with aggression and violence. I had grown up with her father, Slim—we'd gone through some hell in the streets together.

Slim called me one day to ask me to enroll Pigtail in my karate school to straighten her out because she was getting in deep with a girl gang. "I'm afraid if I don't step in, she's gonna end up locked up or dead, or I'm gonna end up eliminating some people," he said.

When I saw Pigtail arrive at class with Slim, she was hanging out of the car, talking smack to people walking by, her usual self. I knew I'd have to have a sit-down with her because I didn't tolerate bullshit in my martial arts academy. After class, I asked her why she'd joined the gang, especially as she came from a solid family.

She said the gang gave her protection from girls at school who were always picking on her and beating her down. She said it happened so many times she developed that aggressiveness as a defense. But even that did not stop the torment. It only stopped when a group of female gang members befriended her. Once she was accepted into the set, which liked her fiery temper and could use it for its own purposes, the bullying stopped immediately. No one else had ever stuck up for her; her Pops tried, but he never really understood how severe the bullying was and thought it was normal kids' stuff. Because the gang stood up for her, she said she'd be loyal to the homegirls, always.

Pigtail made real progress as she studied martial arts with me for two years. She became an outstanding student and a savage street fighter. She also learned how to control her temper most of the time, but she never was able to break away from her homegirls. Her body was found one night in an abandoned house. She had been beaten, strangled, raped repeatedly, and left on a pile of trash. I had grown to love Pigtail like she was my own, and her death affected me profoundly. Her parents never recovered from the loss of their daughter. They divorced, and her mother later committed suicide. Pigtail's killers were never caught.

» Law Enforcement

Contrary to popular belief, a gang's biggest enemy is not police—it's rival gangs, and sometimes they are their own worst enemy. Nevertheless, staying a step ahead of the "popo" (police) is crucial to a gang's survival. In recent years, law enforcement has developed new tools to crack down on gang activity, forcing gangs to change their modus operandi.

Gang injunctions, which are basically restraining orders restricting gang members from congregating on certain areas such as street corners and with certain people, usually each other, have become a popular way to try to tamp down gang activity. In Los Angeles, more than forty injunctions are in place to control the movements of seventy-plus gang sets, and more are being sought all the time. Violating an injunction can lead to jail time. Conditions of a gang member's parole or probation also often contain prohibitions against congregating with documented gang members, whose names appear on a gang list. Once on the district attorney's official gang member list, it is almost impossible to get off it.

Prosecutors have also sought to toughen penalties on gang members with "enhancements," an additional charge for being a gang member that's added onto a criminal case. An enhancement serves to tack more years on to a prison sentence.

The net effect of these policies has been to change the nature of the game by driving gang activity further underground. Much of gangs' dealings used to be conducted more or less out in the open—on street corners and in parks, making it easier for police to keep track of. Now this activity is much harder to detect.

As the nature of the game has changed, so have gangs' operational procedures. Flexibility and adaptation are part of the game. Like everyone else, gangs now use the Internet and social media. "Safebanging" is a new phenomenon, which is dissing each other on various websites, but it can lead to traditional banging like retaliation shootings and killings.

Latino and Asian gangs are subject to another type of law enforcement—deportation. Over the last twenty years, the government has stepped up deportation of immigrants, both legal and illegal, who commit crimes. This has led to an exportation of the gang problem to countries such as El Salvador and Honduras. Lacking skills or opportunities in third world countries, the deported gang members simply set up shop to do what they know how to do. They quickly find that the poverty in those countries has made them ripe for gang lifestyle and culture.

Miguel was deported to his native El Salvador twenty years ago when he was seventeen. He easily set up a "click," or gang set, with twenty-five kids and started holding up buses and burglarizing houses. The Salvadoran youths looked up to the L.A. homeboys, who brought a level of sophistication and discipline they hadn't seen before. "They treated us like kings," Miguel said. "The girls would come knocking at my door."

The deported gang members also maintain ties with their brothers in the United States, setting up a transnational pipeline of organized crime.

》Leaving the Gang

It's not easy to leave a gang, either physically or, especially, emotionally. The set is often the extent of the member's world, all he has known since adolescence, and is firmly entrenched in his neighborhood. The ties run deep.

Gangs tend to frown upon members leaving. It's in their interest to maintain their membership and members know a lot about the inner workings of the set that leaders want to keep within the circle. But most importantly, they don't like members leaving, because abandoning your homies is considered one of the biggest forms of disrespect. To turn your back on your set is like saying all this was a bunch of bullshit.

Gangs don't make leaving easy, although it is not forbidden in the way it used to be—the cause of a green light, or hit, being put on the person, for example. Some sets allow jump-outs as an exit ritual—the person must endure a savage beatdown in order to leave. Gangs are also more inclined to let members leave if they've put in the work or prison time and are well respected, retiring from active duty, so to speak. Another way out is the individual who doesn't want to be a part of the life any more but has agreed to stay in the community and contribute to it, for example, by working with the homies' children in programs that teach self-empowerment, life skills, and academics.

Members who leave must construct new lives for themselves, new relationships, free of the gang influence. It's not easy to just walk away. It's vital they have somewhere to walk to, preferably a new city or state, and something to replace the gang with, like a job and family. Many try to leave and end up falling back in or maintaining some type of bond with the set.

It's virtually impossible to talk someone out of leaving a gang. They leave when they are ready, often because of some major life event, such as the death of someone close or, particularly for women, becoming a parent. For some, that leads to some type of spiritual epiphany that enables them to turn themselves around.

I return to the story of Tony that I started this chapter with. After the shoot-out and his disappearance, I received a letter from Saudi Arabia. It was from Tony, who said he had moved there. Three years later he called me out of the blue. He told me he had become a "man of God" whose mission was now about saving lives. As I put the phone down, I thought back to the shootout. Losing that soldier close to him and seeing his own life at risk was probably what had turned Tony around. It had to reach that extent before he was able to see the destruction he was causing, not only to others but also to himself. But that is not unusual. Because their lifestyle involves taking so many risks and danger, the bottom they have to hit is lower than most people's and may be an accumulation of events.

In the case of Miguel it wasn't being deported, doing a stretch in a Salvadoran prison, nor even blowing off a hand with a grenade full of nails that changed his life. It was an addiction to crack cocaine that led him into a rehab sponsored by the Catholic Church, where he finally decided he'd had enough. "I regret twelve bad years of my existence, twelve years that I ruined my life," he said. "But I don't blame God for none of that because I chose it."

Understanding the gang mindset—and not judging it—is the crucial foundation to intervention work.

2 LICENSE TO OPERATE: GAINING STREET CREDIBILITY

Beatdown had been blasted with three shots in the torso and two in the head while he was standing on the corner with his fellow Crips. He died in a pool of blood on the sidewalk at the age of twenty-two.

Beatdown got his nickname from his fists. He rarely lost a fight, even when he was up against two or three guys. But fists are no match for .45 caliber bullets.

As far as gang shootings go, it was a pretty regular one—a retaliation drive-by, assumed to be perpetrated by a set of the Crips' archrivals, the Bloods, for an incursion into their territory. At least, that was the word on the street. There was also a rumor that he had been set up.

The funeral was to be held several days later at a mega church in South L.A. that handles a lot of gang funerals. Gang funerals are real events in the neighborhood; homies have to be laid to rest with the proper level of respect. But gang funerals aren't just about mourning. They can be a prime target for a move by a rival set, an opportunity to do major damage because of the large gathering of members of the opposing gang, including the shot callers who don't often show their faces. They can also fuel the collective desire for revenge on the part of the victimized set, especially if the taking of the victim's life was not seen as justified.

For years, funerals were off limits to gang warfare, but that has changed in the last decade and a half. Funerals are now considered open season in many neighborhoods as a hardened mindset has taken hold that says no place is exempt and sets must protect their territory at all costs.

Beatdown, always recognizable by his T-shirt with the universal power sign of a raised fist, was well liked, not just in his hood but also in rival hoods, because he was known to be fair on the street. He had a rare integrity within the game that crossed traditional gang lines. His funeral was going to attract a wide circle of Crips, homeboys, and others. The problem was the location of the church—smack in the middle of turf claimed by three rival sets.

In cases like these, negotiating a pass or "stand-down" with the local shot callers would be standard operating procedure as a sign of respect. The set holding the funeral normally requests a four- or five-hour pass to drive through the rival neighborhoods, attend the funeral, and drive out. As long as there are no wars or exceptional bad blood, funeral passes are usually granted. But for some reason, this got overlooked for Beatdown's funeral.

Minutes from War

It was one of those typical Southern California afternoons—a cloudless, bright blue sky that seemed at odds with the somber nature of the event at hand. A caravan of thirty-plus vehicles, a mix of cherried-out lowriders and high-end luxury cars, waxed to a mirror shine with gleaming chrome rims flashing in the sun, slowly followed the hearse along the five mile-long route from the funeral home to the church. The procession was accompanied by two point cars, which sped up and down the street to make sure no interlopers broke the line and to block intersections at red lights so the mourners' cars could pass unhindered.

The local sets all knew about the funeral and had posted lookouts on the roofs of apartment buildings to see and be seen. They were there to send a message loud and clear about who the hood belonged to and to relay information about the procession back to headquarters.

The procession arrived at the church and the funeral began. The place was packed. People kept arriving well after the preacher started lamenting yet another senseless death of a young man as his bereaved mother sobbed. Outside, another type of action was under way.

Bloods soldiers and members of other rival sets had rolled up in their riders and formed a circle around the church. They were infuriated at the blatant snub this Crips set had given them by passing through their turf without permission. This was a major sign of disrespect and could not go unanswered. Meanwhile, inside the church, tension was building between members of other rival sets.

Despite the fact they were all friends of Beatdown, there was heavy-duty mad-dogging going down.

A former Blood, Fist was now a PCITI gang interventionist. He'd been a close friend of Beatdown's even though they belonged to rival sets, and the family had invited him and a couple of his crew to the funeral. Beatdown's hood had given him a pass to attend because they respected his relationship with their homie. Fist saw the lowriders assembling outside the church. Inside, he noticed the staredowns. His gut seized up—something major was about to pop off the minute the Crips walked out of the service.

He jumped on the phone, first to me and then to a couple interventionists who had been Bloods shot callers. It was a high-alert situation. A move on a funeral would result in a bloodbath, bring heat on the hood, and spark untold retaliation for moving on an enemy at a time when he was down. A plan of action had to be put in place immediately. We rushed to the church, knowing we only had as much time as the funeral service lasted.

Our team started to work the crowd. Interventionists who had once belonged to rival sets walked side by side to send a message of peace and unity as I organized a team to form a buffer around the church. The negotiations were intense as interventionists appealed to the gang members' sense of honor over their wounded pride.

"We gotta stand down here, homie. This is what Beatdown would've wanted. Beatdown stood for unity, bro. We gotta honor his memory. We can't disrespect his life by starting a war over his funeral."

The message was not well received by many. "They disrespected us. We can't let this go. They gotta pay," the younger gang members kept saying.

It was a tense forty-five minutes of back and forth. We didn't know which side was going to win. But the younger guys were reined in by the O.G.s, who eventually realized if chaos erupted at the funeral, it could be years before any kind of peace could be restored. The pressure worked. Everyone stood down, although many were not happy, and they left the church by the time the service ended. The procession proceeded to the cemetery unharmed.

》The Importance of Street Cred

The key to the success of this engagement: interventionists with validated LTOs—licenses to operate. In the most basic terms, LTO is street credibility, your reputation as someone who can be trusted, lives by his or her word, and has serious "throwdown," courage, and backbone. The more people who have validated your track record in the community, the wider your LTO and the more effective interventionist you are. LTO is the one of the most important pillars of hard-core violence intervention. Without it, intervention simply cannot work.

Earning the respect and trust of others is important in any venue in life, but in gang life it's crucial. When reputation is all you've got, you've got to maintain it at all costs. One act of disrespect like rivals rolling through your turf to a funeral, or a perceived slight like an underling looking the wrong way at a shot caller's girlfriend, can cost lives. That's why respect and trust in the form of an LTO is vital in gang intervention.

Players won't deal with anyone who doesn't come with that calling card because it would be lowering them to an inferior standard. They've got to know that who they're dealing with can be trusted so they'll come out looking good and keep the respect of others. LTO does not come easy. It is earned on the street through actions, not bluster and bravado, and can take years to build. One misstep can wipe out an LTO in minutes and can cost lives.

We had a war going on between four hoods deep in South L.A. The cycle of revenge had been going on for some time and the community was getting tired. Kids couldn't even get to school without cell phones and watches being jacked by gang members asserting their control over territory. The breaking point came when an eleven-year-old boy was killed by stray gunfire as he walked to school, a block from his home. His mother was standing on the front porch and witnessed her son's death.

I got called in by a middle-school principal, who asked me if I could do something to get the gangs to stop warring around the school. My LTO in this area was weak because of the lack of work put in there, so I utilized my network. I called five interventionists who had LTOs with the various sets involved to get everyone to a mediation session. One interventionist, J.J., offered to bring two shot callers from the set that controlled the largest amount of territory. I readily agreed; I needed to get that set to the table.

We met in a local community center that was declared neutral turf. After all the participants were patted down—no weapons were allowed—we gathered around a large table. But when J.J.'s two shot callers sat down, I sensed right away something was off. The reps from the other sets seemed uneasy dealing with them, but to some extent, that's normal when enemies confront one another. I dismissed my gut feeling, told my people to keep an eye on things, and we got down to business. Over the next three hours, we reached no agreement except to agree to return for another session, which was a baby step forward, but a step forward. During the second meeting, we finally hammered out a stand-down of three days of no gunfire. This was an important advance and I was pleased.

A day later, however, I got a call from a shot caller in one of the sets. "Aquil, what's this bullshit about some damn stand-down? Our people didn't agree to this."

Surprised, I explained that reps from his hood were at the meeting. He asked who they were. I told him J.J. and the two homies.

It turned out that J.J.'s "shot callers" were in fact underlings with no decision-making power in their set. They were busters, claiming reputations they did not have. The stand-down was suddenly off because it had never really been on. The situation was now worse than ever. The one set felt like they'd been played by the other sets to look like the bad guys because they would go ahead

and unknowingly violate the stand-down they had supposedly agreed to. That would give the three other hoods the excuse to go after them. The three other neighborhoods were pissed off that underlings had been sent to deal with them, meaning they didn't merit the respect and ranking of the real shot callers.

It took me four months to get the sets back to the table and get a real stand-down in place. J.J. was long gone. He wasn't getting a second chance from me. Obviously, he did not have sufficient LTO to deliver the decision makers to the table and he wasn't honest enough to admit it. His dishonesty had caused more people to get hurt.

》 How Do You Get It?

The big question I always get about LTO is "how do you get it?" Many interventionists are former gang members, so they start out with a certain amount of LTO with their hoods. That inside LTO has to be earned, too. In the upside-down values of gang culture, respect is often gained by doing the worst, most undesirable things—the dirty work. Doing prison time, and more importantly how you do the time—holding your own and keeping up your rep at all costs—is another way gang members earn respect from peers. Not snitching to law enforcement to save yourself is another way. It's not just one thing. It's a continual display of loyalty to the gang that earns high-ranked LTO.

I get calls from all kinds of people who want access to gangs and the neighborhoods they control: social workers, parks and recreation employees, city maintenance crews, police and fire personnel, businesses, sociologists and psychologists, journalists, and filmmakers.

Gang members don't respond well to outsiders. They are suspicious and mistrustful, sometimes because of the criminal nature of their activities, sometimes because they know the outsiders want something from the culture, and because they come from an environment where official people mean trouble. But the main factor is that they regard their community as theirs, and they are the gate-keepers.

Neighborhood "ownership" is not a concept that people from middle-class communities can easily get their heads around. It just doesn't happen in suburban housing developments with manicured lawns and tricycles in the driveways. But in gang zones, it's so serious that people lose their lives over it. Turf control is a critical part of gang culture. The worst thing you can do is ignore the gang or dismiss it. Gang members will make it impossible for you to operate in that community. The bottom line is you need to establish a credible LTO to move in these neighborhoods. There are a couple ways to get that.

Meeting Needs

Gangs exist in neighborhoods with a lot of needs. The first step is to find out what local people need and offer something toward that. If you are there only to take, you will not get cooperation from the shot callers, or anyone else, and can even get heavy-duty harassment.

Magic Johnson announced a big plan to build a multimillion-dollar multiplex movie theatre in the Crenshaw area of South L.A. It was a big deal back in 1994—it was all over the news and won a lot of praise from city leaders as a sign of urban revitalization. The local community was pleased, too—it was going to bring jobs to a community that badly needed them.

The company broke ground on construction, but the expected jobs didn't materialize. The brothers watched angrily as union construction workers paraded in to the site every morning—all outsiders. They felt that all Magic's rhetoric about investing in urban communities was just that—rhetoric.

They made their feelings known in a silent, but not so subtle, way. Every morning a couple dozen brothers would go down to the construction site and surround it, striking the gang stance—arms crossed, legs apart, and eyes trained unblinkingly on the workers. They said nothing, did nothing, just glared—the classic gang tactic of mad-dogging designed to intimidate. It worked—they unsettled the workers and the foreman contacted the management.

I got called by a fellow PCITI peacekeeper, T Rogers, who'd been handling the issue well but needed some backup to deal with Magic's team. They had requested a meeting to find out what was going on. He knew I had a solid LTO with corporate "suits," so he wanted me there. "We need to make sure we come out of there with something," T said. I agreed.

We met one morning in a local coffee shop with Magic and his top guy. The four of us squeezed in around one of those little round tables. And it was a squeeze. I didn't realize how big Magic was till I sat next to him.

Magic wanted to find a solution. His concern was that if he hired brothers from the hood, they wouldn't show up and really work. T and I went back to the brothers and laid down the rules—they had to show up for work on time; listen to the foreman; no stealing from the job site; if someone got fired, there'd be no retaliation; and so on. The brothers agreed. It took a couple meetings, but eventually Magic agreed to hire about twenty-five men at union wages. The soldiers and the community were satisfied. That movie theatre never saw as much as a smear of graffiti.

Outsiders who want something from a neighborhood have to do something for the neighborhood in return. When a movie was filming in a South L.A. neighborhood, the director employed gang members as extras. Owners of corner liquor and grocery stores often offer tabs to families so they can keep food on the table until they get their next food stamps or welfare check. In return, they don't get robbed, vandalized, or graffiti-tagged.

Some people might look askance at this quid-pro-quo tactic, but in the inner-city, where opportunities are rare and people feel ignored and disenfranchised, it's a survival strategy, as well as a demand to be taken into account.

Connecting to LTO

Another way for an outsider to get LTO is to connect with someone who has it. That person can provide an entrée into the community on the basis of his own LTO, a validation of sorts off his name. If the outsider doesn't live up to what is promised, both the validator and the outsider will have to answer for it.

Pete Carroll, who was then the coach of the University of Southern California Trojan's football team, wanted to talk to gang members after seeing how violence affected his players' lives, families, and communities. He wanted to do something about it, but first he needed to understand what he was dealing with.

Through mutual connections, Pete hooked up with me and another interventionist, Bo Taylor, a close friend of mine. With some of our crew, we would meet Pete at ten at night, and after leaving his black Mercedes in a parking lot, drive him into housing projects and gang hot spots so he could talk to validated street soldiers and authenticated shot callers. He wanted to find out what motivated them, what it would take to quell the violence. He was so fired up that he'd bound out of the car and dart into the projects on his own. We had to run after him to rein him in, explaining that gang members didn't appreciate strangers showing up on their own, even if it was Pete Carroll.

Many of the gangsters knew who Pete was and were surprised to see him in the hood, wondering right away what he wanted. But Bo and I would pave the way, telling them he was really interested in learning about their lives because he wanted to do something to help them. Once they felt Pete didn't want anything and sensed his genuineness, they opened up, softening because he took the time and trouble to venture onto their turf just to listen to them.

We went all over L.A. Pete stayed out talking to guys until 2:00 or 3:00 AM. He always came back moved by the squalor of the living conditions that he saw and the hopelessness that he heard from youths about their lives. He'd say that as long as their vision is not to live past twenty-five, they'll find a way to fulfill that. He brought them to Trojans practices a couple times so they could see there was life and hope beyond the hood.

Pete kept his word. He was a lead founder of A Better LA, a nonprofit organization that funded a group of gang interventionists and got my PCITI off the ground. Now head coach with the Seattle Seahawks, he's doing the same thing in that city with a new organization called A Better Seattle. Pete called me to train the outreach workers in that city, and I then got called into neighboring Tacoma to assist there too. That's all a bottom-line result of possessing an authenticated LTO.

» Maintaining LTO

An LTO is like a driver's license. It expires. You have to keep doing the work to keep it current. There's a constant flow of people cycling in and out of street gangs as people get sentenced to prison, get killed, or drop out for one reason or another. A new crop of recruits is always right behind them. So you have to maintain that LTO by being consistent in your words and actions.

When I hold my gang-intervention training course, the Professional Community Intervention Training Institute, my leadership team and I personally vet the candidates who sign up for the class. One of the things I look for is the LTO that individuals have on the street, but another key is their sense of personal integrity and commitment to the work. If candidates do not have that, they will not be able to maintain and expand their LTO, which will make them an ineffective interventionist and reflect badly on the PCITI.

My own LTO has a lot of age and weight to it. It goes back to the days when I was a young militant in the Black Power movement in the late sixties. I was a part of some of the country's most radical and feared groups of that era—the Black Panther Party, the Nation, and the Black Student Union. Many members of these groups, including myself, came from the old street gangs, like the Slausons, the Businessmen, the Bounty Hunters, and the Gladiators.

As Black Power militants, our aim was to lift the black community out of oppression—violence, drugs, pimping, prostitution, and other vices that were keeping our community in the ghetto. We took pride in fighting the establishment through rallies and marches, and with fists and guns when we had to. When we got arrested, our unwritten rule was we did not go down without a fight. There was many a time when I got carted off to jail busted up with a swollen eye, big bruises, and one time, a broken arm and wrist. Every wound was a badge of honor to us. We had other unwritten rules, like you did not snitch to the cops—ever. As with today's gangs, the punishment for snitching was being "blacklisted," losing all street cred, and according to the importance of the information that was snitched, serious injury or even death.

With my training and skill in firearms and improvised weaponry and being a master of martial arts, my main role in the movement was regulation and enforcement. I handled the business of disciplining individuals who broke the rules and stepping to adversaries who disrespected our organizations. I mediated crises and conflicts with those who didn't appreciate what our organizations were doing.

In the early seventies, as the Black Power movement was slowly crushed by the FBI, law enforcement, and the establishment; street gangs like the Crips and Bloods sprang up in its place. Drugs became their lifeblood. Many disillusioned militants joined the gangs and used the power in gangs to participate in destructive activity, or got hooked on heroin and other narcotics that were flooding into our community, or did both. I did neither. I stuck to the principle of the Black Power movement—drugs and violence destroy our community, and we couldn't partake in the vices we were trying to eradicate. I continued the work I started as a militant, which laid the foundation for my community intervention.

My background had already given me street skills, as well as a reputation with many gang members as a no-nonsense, uncompromising diehard militant who was not to be fucked with. I continued my mission of ending the self-destructive behaviors plaguing our community. Working in the hard-core gang environment was an easy transition for me because of where I came from and what I had been through.

» Different Types of LTO

Gangs are highly localized and are rooted along racial and ethnic lines. To build an effective intervention team, you need male and female interventionists who have LTOs with a variety of gangs. LTO that crosses ethnic and geographic borders is not usual, but it can be done.

I got called in by a parents' group at a school in central L.A. to help with a gang problem at a nearby housing project. The caveat was that this gang was out of my normal sphere of operation—they were Cambodian. Like many immigrant groups, the Cambodians had formed a gang as protection against the black and Latino gangs in the area. There was a lot of tension among the gangs and resentment from local residents who saw the Cambodians as taking their jobs at nearby factories. Cambodian families, meanwhile, were afraid of the new gangs and didn't like younger kids being recruited.

I didn't have one iota of an LTO with the Cambodian community. I wasn't sure what the hell I was going to do. It was a very insular community. Many of the parents didn't speak English, and they were very protective of their kids against any outside influence. The kids were suspicious of outsiders given the problems they had encountered.

As I drove into the project of low-lying, pancake apartment buildings, the set members stood and mad-dogged me. I could hear them talking as they stared me down hard. "Who the fuck is this fool? I know he ain't about to come up in here. Asshole better back the fuck up."

I knew the look and had heard the talk many times before. It didn't faze me. Still, I had to be a little more cautious than usual since I didn't fully know what I was dealing with, but I knew I had to come on strong. I did the classic gang acknowledgement—a quick nod of the head without a smile or words—a sign of respect, but not trying to be friends. One or two returned the nod, most didn't.

I started meeting with parents at the community center in the housing project. Knowing the respect for elders in the Asian culture, I needed to get the parents on my side, so I decided to tackle them first. The parents, who came from a culture where children did what they were told, were bewildered at the changes in their kids—talking back, blatantly ignoring what their parents told them. They didn't know what to do. I talked to them through younger kids who translated, which also helped spread the word about what I was doing among the youth in the project. Still, it took time to win their trust—a lot longer than I expected—and I wasn't sure I was going to get anywhere.

Eventually, three boys, who were curious as to what I was doing, befriended me. Through the basic LTO they provided me, I was able to reach out to the gang members and talk to them about recruiting younger kids. Then a mother invited me to her house for a meal. I immediately accepted. I don't know what the hell she put in front of me, but after making sure it did not contain meat (I've been a vegetarian for decades), I ate it. That broke the ice. More parents invited me into their homes, even to family gatherings and birthday parties. One lady gave me a Cambodian necklace.

When the gang members saw that I wasn't going away and I wasn't there to come down on them, they opened up to me for help with some serious problems. A black gang had green-lighted a Cambodian boy—they had put out a hit on him—and a Latino gang was picking on two boys so severely they couldn't step outside the project, not even to go to school, without being jacked and harassed. There was no real reason for these actions. The Cambodians were simply easy marks.

I negotiated a stand-down between the Cambodians and the black and Latino gangs. Even that was not easy. The Cambodians felt I was favoring the blacks and Latinos. I had to take extra care to make sure I was fair and equal to all players. That was the real turning point. After that, tensions slowly simmered down to the stage where I was able to phase out my intervention work there. It was a long process, about four years all told.

Broad LTO

To be truly effective, interventionists must possess LTOs beyond the borders of their own people and neighborhoods. You have to be able to cross rival lines and be accepted by the people who were once your sworn enemies, including law enforcement. Larger LTOs come from doing work constructive to the general community, community stakeholders, and political and public safety entities. It is earned the same way it is with gang members—keeping your word and coming through, being neutral and fair to both sides. As you start working on a wider scale, your reputation as someone who can deliver—or not—will spread and will help you do your work.

I have expanded my own LTO to the very power structure I once fought against, such as City Hall, emergency responders, and law enforcement, and with people I never thought I'd be rubbing shoulders with, like philanthropists and businessmen. To do that, I had to put aside old prejudices.

I was assisting a city councilman on gang issues in his district and helping him on security. I accompanied him to many of his public appearances. Sometimes I'd catch myself at some of these ribbon cuttings and ground breakings and shake my head at what I was doing. After my years in the Black Power movement, I had real disdain for politicians. I couldn't believe I was actually collaborating with one, but I knew the councilman was trying to do positive things for the community. Working around him, I started to see that moving within the establishment could help me get ahead. He'd introduce me to official types as his go-to guy on gangs and violence, and eventually people sought me out on their own for advice on gang, youth aggression, and public-safety issues. That was the door-opener to getting a contract to conduct my youth-development program in fifteen schools. I saw that you have to move beyond your old hostilities to help you accomplish what you need to accomplish. You have to keep expanding that LTO. I continue to do that today.

LTO is the best and most essential tool for dealing with gangs. It is what makes one interventionist stand out from the others. But there's no easy formula for it. A lot of it relies on an individual's skill at building rapport with people and also the ability to be open, reliable, and trustworthy.

3 THE YELLOW TAPE: MANAGING THE CRIME SCENE

It had been one of those pressure-cooker summer days where the air was as still as cement and the asphalt seemed to fry everything on its surface. But dusk had finally arrived, giving this Southeast Los Angeles neighborhood some mercy from the daylong baking sun. Residents eagerly moved out of their stifling non-air-conditioned homes to take advantage of twilight's coolness. Elders sat in chairs on porches exchanging neighborhood gossip as they kept a diligent eye on young ones running amok on the sidewalk and front yards. The tantalizing aroma of barbecue wafted over the street as fathers tossed meat on backyard grills while in kitchens, mothers prepared potato salad and other fixings for the weekend "cue."

As sunset settled in, the harmony was suddenly shattered by the screech of tires, then several firecracker-loud pops. An eerie moment of silence overtook the neighborhood as residents stood stock still, waiting for the inevitable screams of grief they knew all too well would follow.

The drive-by had wounded three people, two critically and one slightly. An eleven-year-old girl was the worst off with multiple gunshots to the upper body and neck. A seventeen-year-old male had also sustained a life-threatening bullet wound to his femoral artery in the thigh.

My squad and I happened to be just blocks away from the scene. We heard the shots and zipped in the direction of the gunfire. When we arrived, I spotted a fire engine down the block at the corner and was glad help was already there. A couple homies ran over and gave us the lowdown on what just transpired, then started pointing and yelling angrily that the firefighters had been on the corner for about five minutes but refused to come to the scene.

I looked down the street, wondering what was going on. One firefighter, who was holding what seemed to be a first aid kit, stood nervously by the front of the truck, looking like he wanted to rush over but couldn't for some reason, while the others just sat in the vehicle staring at everyone.

Neighbors were gathering and the crowd was getting big. People were waving to the firefighters, shouting frantically that the gunshot victims were bleeding to death, but the fire crew would not budge. Frustration and anger were mounting. One elderly lady marched down to the vehicle and got into it with the captain.

"What the hell are you doing? We got people dying on the street and your asses are sitting in this truck. Go do your damn job!" she yelled.

"We're waiting for police protection. I can't jeopardize my crew, the shooter could still be in the area," the captain answered.

"That's what you bastards are paid to do!" she fired back.

A police squad car, red lights flashing and sirens blasting, rocketed into the street, followed by five more police cars. After a thirty-second conversation with police, the fire crew finally sped to the victims, who were lying in spreading pools of blood, but there was not much they could do—the victims died. The delay most likely didn't make a difference, the victims were too severely injured, but to the community it seemed like unforgivable neglect. They hurled a non-stop barrage of threats and insults at the firefighters. "You let them die! All you had to do was give them some help, but because they were from this neighborhood, you let them die!" "You're going to get yours!" "We better not see you on the streets!" "Watch your backs. You can die just like we can!"

My team and I knew we had to calm the crowd, which was threatening to spin out of control. We started working to move people back, telling them to let the paramedics do their job. But the cops didn't appreciate our efforts.

"We don't need your help. You need to get your asses out of the area. It's already hot enough as it is, and we don't need no more bullshit. This is an active crime scene," an officer told us. I replied we were trained interventionists and knew basic crime-scene protocol.

"I don't give a hoot about what the hell you think you know. You and your people need to get your behinds up out of here before I have you arrested," he ordered, in a typical display of law enforcement's early mentality toward interventionists.

I told my people to stand down and we hesitantly backed off. The crowd grew agitated as the news went around that the critically injured victims had died. Despite the flare-up of some tempers, the crowd on the whole stayed contained, milling around on the street for hours. Eventually most left, although a group of teenagers stayed late into the night. Many local residents felt the victims could have survived if they had received quicker assistance from the fire department.

Whether this is true or not we'll never know, but the incident left a lot of distrust and ill will in the community toward fire personnel. It became clear to me that police and firefighters needed to be more sensitive to the community, and the community needed to know how public safety officials worked. Interventionists are the ideal link between the two—we have the community trust, and with our training, we understand public-safety protocol.

Much of interventionists' work starts at the crime scene, and this is often where the most delicate handling is needed. Scenes of shootings and homicides are charged with high emotion, particularly when young people are victims. Parents are openly grieving, neighbors are shocked, homeboys are angry, crowds of onlookers gather. In the midst of that, paramedics, police, and coroner's investigators must do their job and can seem unsympathetic in the community's eyes.

The interventionist plays two key roles here: crowd control, which allows officials to do their jobs efficiently and prevents chaos from breaking out, and rumor control, which can head off possible retaliation by the victim's homeboys and provides information to relatives who want answers as to what happened to their loved one. (Rumor control will be addressed in detail in the next chapter.) The interventionist must also deal directly with firefighters and delicately with police officials, providing both a buffer and a liaison between them and the community.

» First on the Scene

Because we live in the neighborhood, interventionists are often on the scene before first responders arrive. This one of the reasons why I train my peacekeepers in "street trauma," first aid, and CPR, as well electronic paddle use. Street trauma first aid expands regular first aid procedures to include tending to mas-

sive bullet, knife, and blunt-force wounds. Those seconds after a person is shot can mean the difference as to whether the incident is a homicide or not.

Nikko De, a PCITI interventionist and instructor, was deejaying one night at a packed sweet-sixteen house party on the west side of Los Angeles when the sound of loud pops broke through the reggae tune he was spinning. The partygoers scrambled and dropped to the floor. The gunfire stopped, and Nikko instructed everybody to crawl out the back door while he cautiously checked the front yard. "I saw five or six people bleeding, and nobody was really helping them. People were just standing there, taking pictures and videos with their phones. I ran out," he said.

Nikko made tourniquets with T-shirts and jeans on bullet wounds in legs, feet, and backs, then his attention was drawn to a guy on the porch who was gasping for air, his mouth working soundlessly. There was no sign of blood, but Nikko gave him CPR to stabilize his breathing. Paramedics arrived, and Nikko directed them to the guy on the porch who was still having difficulty breathing. They cut off his clothes, leaving him in his boxers, but detected no bullet wound. They concluded he was drunk or high and set about transporting the other victims to the hospital.

Nikko's instinct and interventionist training told him something was wrong. "A girl told me he'd been at the gate when the shooters came up and he told people 'they got me.' I checked him again, flipping him over, then I saw something right between his buttocks and spine." Nikko touched the entry wound; blood spurted. He called the paramedics back, and they got the man to the hospital. The final toll of this gang-reprisal shooting: one man dead, one paralyzed from the waist down, and five injured.

The early arrival of interventionists on the scene also allows them to gather preliminary information to give first responders, who must evaluate a situation involving gunfire and aggression before going in because of possible danger to themselves. In many cities, including Los Angeles, fire department policy gives personnel the right to decide if a scene is too unsafe for them to enter.

If so, they can "stage," or wait for police assistance, before going in, which is what transpired in the situation detailed earlier in the chapter. Most often fire personnel will engage, but it is a determination based on the fire captain's evaluation of the crew's safety. It's a tricky decision that can go either way. Officers who come from the neighborhoods or have worked in the area for some time are usually more comfortable about going in while others may be more hesitant.

Interventionists can give emergency responders and paramedics the quick lowdown on the scene: if the shooter is still there, how many shots have been fired, if the shots came from different locations, if there are any incendiary devices in the area. The answers help emergency workers assess the situation—if there are multiple gunmen, or the possibility of ongoing gunfire or crossfire that they could get caught in, for example. "Interventionists play a critical role whether we stage or not," says L.A. Assistant Fire Chief Kwame Cooper. "If they're first on the scene, they can go up to the fire truck and say, 'We've scoped it out. It's safe.'"

Seeing victims get rapid emergency treatment helps assure the community that the best service is being provided, which goes a long way to keeping people calm. As word of the shooting spreads, people start congregating. With the high distrust of uniforms in inner-city neighborhoods, it doesn't take much to get people riled up when there's a body in the street, especially if drink and drugs are added to the mix.

Brent Burton, a captain in the Los Angeles County Fire Department, says he's been berated by hostile bystanders, colleagues have been threatened verbally and with guns, fire trucks have been shot at. "Crowds get irate and anxious, and they take it out on the paramedics. They think we don't work fast enough.

Folks just see blue uniforms and badges and think we're just an extension of the police. I even have my crew wear helmets and yellow jackets so we can be differentiated."

》Crowd Control

Crowd control forms a crucial element of handling an emotional scene. It's an essential tool of the professional interventionist.

A key function of crowd control is ensuring that people stay out of what is known as the "immediate danger to life" (IDL) area, or hot zone, where the crime occurred, so emergency responders can do their job unhindered and trace evidence remains uncontaminated for use in law-enforcement investigations.

Below is an illustration of the three "zones" comprising a typical crime scene, ranging from the most dangerous (hot) area to the safest (cold) area.

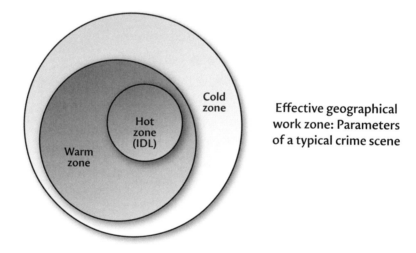

Effective geographical work zone: Parameters of a typical crime scene

Another important function of crowd control is simply giving out correct information so onlookers understand what the paramedics and police are doing and why. People are often alarmed, for instance, when they see a body twitching under the white sheet. They think the victim is still alive and feel that the paramedics and cops gave up the person for dead without trying to save him.

Interventionists step in to explain that the body moves because of interior gases building up. Likewise, bystanders get angry when emergency workers cut off a victim's clothes, because it looks like they don't care about the victim. We explain that they're looking for additional bullet wounds, and cutting off clothing is the fastest way to do that when a person could be hemorrhaging internally.

Los Angeles police Sgt. Curtis Woodle, who's been a cop for three decades—two in the South L.A. gang unit—says controlling crowds is a vital function at shooting scenes. Before interventionists regularly rolled up at incidents, bystanders always got heated out of a feeling of being disrespected by officials. "The interventionist can explain what's going on. As a police officer, I can't do that because of the mistrust," he says.

Interventionists can help sensitize officials to the community, too. People would often get upset at seeing a body lying in the street for hours as forensic analysts worked around it. After interventionists, victims' relatives, and community stakeholders complained repeatedly and asked for more respect for the victims, the Los Angeles Police Department started setting up tents around bodies so they are not visible.

Once medical workers are on the scene, interventionists form a crucial buffer between them and an emotional community. They can find a family member if an identification is needed or get information such as the victim's medical history or medications, relieving paramedics from the stress of dealing with panicked relatives.

Another aspect of crowd control is getting out the basic facts of the crime to the community right away to quash rumors that can inflame emotions. Sgt. Woodle recalls one instance where police had chased a suspect into a housing development. During the ensuing scuffle, the suspect shot himself in the head in front of his mother, who happened to be a well-known interventionist in the community. A crowd gathered outside heard the gunshot and believed cops had shot the young man. They started throwing rocks and bottles at the sheriff's deputies and police. "It became very intense, it was going down. The captain got the mother to come and talk to the crowd to tell them what happened. They ended up dispersing themselves," Woodle says. "I've seen interventionists quiet down a rough crowd just by telling them, 'wait till you get the information.' It works."

When engaging with interventionists at crime scenes, Los Angeles police give them the same facts about a murder as they give to news reporters, no more, no less. Interventionists can also function as reporters on their own. By getting to the aftermath of a shooting before the yellow tape goes up, they can visually document the scene without disturbing any evidence. That personal observation can also be used to counter exaggerated rumors that may spring up later.

Crowd control also comprises the physical act of moving people. This might involve taking one or more rabble-rousers to the side and talking them down or dispersing a crowd, courteously moving it back, or protecting a spokesman addressing the people. We do this through specific crowd-control techniques. The procedures most often used are:

- Encirclement: This involves deploying a team to form a circular perimeter around the crowd. The team members gradually move in and enclose the group, and then start moving in the desired direction, thus shifting the crowd with them.

- Channeling: This creates an aisle for the crowd to move through. Team members position themselves on either side and at one end of the group, then slowly nudge people through the established channel.

- Funneling: This is used to control the number and placement of people in a gathering. The rear of the crowd is relatively open, but at the front end only a small opening is created. Supervisors thus have more direction over people.

- Isolation: This involves breaking up a crowd into smaller groups and isolating them from each other to defuse tempers and high-running emotion. This is a delicate maneuver that requires a lot of manpower since each group requires a team.

With all of the techniques, it is essential that they be carried out with firmness but not force. Team members must address the crowd respectfully and tell people what they are trying to do. Residents are more likely to go along with direction if it comes from people like themselves and if they understand what is going on and why.

» Dealing with Law Enforcement

Crime scenes often involve a tightrope situation for interventionists because we must possess a practical working relationship with some law-enforcement officers in full view of the community, but let me stress unquestionably that we are not collaborators, investigators, or informants, nor can we be perceived as such. We do not provide information for police to make arrests with. The interventionist's role is more of a community liaison, a neutral go-between who, for instance, police might go to for help in moving back crowd or to give the crowd accurate information about what is transpiring.

But for many residents of urban neighborhoods, cops are the sworn enemy. Even talking to an officer can earn someone the reputation of being a snitch. Creating a workable balance between maintaining the respect of the community amid traditional hostility toward law enforcement is essential to being a good interventionist.

It took me a long time to overcome my own disgust toward cops. Having been a part of the Black Power movement and some of its most militant groups, I had seen plenty of racism against blacks and Latinos by police. I had witnessed the water hoses turned on my people. I had endured countless beatings by men in uniform for no other reason than they could. Believe me, I had no love for the boys in blue. But as I matured, I came to realize that not all police were bad. Several of the kids I mentored went into the police force. I met some real sympathetic cops during the investigation of my brother's death.

Working as a firefighter and later as a fire inspector, I got to know police officers on a more-personal basis. I saw there were good cops and bad cops, just like there are good interventionists and bad ones. Now I judge law-enforcement officers individually. If cops provide constructive assistance to the community, they get my full respect, if they don't, I won't deal with them. I tell my guys you can't generalize. You have to leave the past where it is and move forward, because a working relationship with officers who have proven themselves to be an asset to the communities they serve is necessary for the success of the work.

The same goes for cops. Many police officers are skeptical of interventionists because of the criminal backgrounds many of us have. Curtis Woodle recalled that the first time he spoke to my peacekeeper training class, he was not only apprehensive but didn't think he could accomplish much. "I walked in and saw these were all the troublemakers. I thought, 'why am I even here?' But then we started talking, and I started to respect the men in the room, regardless of their past. I talked to them as men. We were both trying to do the same thing— save lives."

There are some general rules. Police officers need to know the appropriate ways to approach interventionists—don't roll up in a squad car and yell out if they're on the corner with a bunch of homeboys, avoid giving them special treatment, don't shake hands or slap backs at a crime scene. Being seen as buddies with cops can damage the interventionist's LTO in the community. A respected professional relationship is all that can be asked for.

Different interventionist groups have different protocols for dealing with law enforcement. Some interventionist groups, particularly those that are funded with public money, can be required to report to a police contact at the crime scene. Privately funded groups, like mine, have no such directive and are more flexible.

We will work with any agency who shares our goal of saving lives, preventing injuries, and restoring communities. We won't have a relationship with officers or others who have proven themselves to be dogmatic, vengeful, hateful, and hurtful to the people we serve. The bottom line is respectful communication without judgment on either side. Both parties must know their boundaries, understand how each other works, and hold each other accountable based on skills and protocols, not personalities. We do not take sides or work for anybody. We remain neutral and answer only to the communities we serve.

» Dealing with Paramedics and Firefighters

The 911 call came in from an area of South L.A. called "the Jungle" because of its rows upon rows of cookie-cutter apartment buildings that are almost impossible to navigate without a local resident. Paramedics were met with a hail of gunfire aimed directly at them from a second-story window. The shooter got off about nine rapid-fire rounds and the medics fled. Worried that emergency responders might not respond to the next 911 call because of that, a group of residents called me in to smooth things over with the paramedics and prevent this from happening again.

I already had a pretty good sense of what probably happened—we had received numerous complaints about a particular emergency-response shift from members of this community, and this was likely some type of reprisal. My first step was to track down the shooter. This was a tiring process with no guarantee of success, but we were lucky. Through peacekeepers from the area, we were able to find the man and confront him. He readily admitted to calling in a fake emergency to lure paramedics into an ambush because he wanted to give them a lesson. Paramedics had been to his apartment several times, and each time, they had been rude and disrespectful. Luckily for the paramedics—and for him, he was an exceptionally bad shot.

We gave the paramedics tips on spotting a potential ambush, if a supposed emergency scene looks too quiet, for example, as well as on seeking the best cover to protect themselves, preferably some type of metal. We also sensitized them to how the community can perceive their actions and demeanor. Sometime later, we heard the man had been arrested and prosecuted for his actions. We played no role in his arrest and were thankful we were not asked to.

I could relate to the man's experience, although not his reaction. When I first started my thirty-plus year career with the Los Angeles Fire Department, I used to get extremely angry at how some firefighters treated poor people. It was a lot different than how they treated residents in more affluent areas. One time, paramedics told an old fragile lady, who was black and lived in a low-income neighborhood, that she was faking the pain she was suffering. "How much drugs have you taken?" one asked her. They didn't ask this of other old ladies of non-color who complained of pain.

My background as a militant made me undaunted to speak up. I'd stop firefighters from dragging dirty, wet hoses across the carpets of modest homes and climbing over old furniture. "This doesn't look like much, but it's all these people got," I told my colleagues angrily. I'd have to step in and neutralize situations when a firefighter looked at somebody the wrong way or said something disrespectful, especially to the homies from the hood. "That badge don't stop no lead, fool," was the response I heard all the time on the street. The firefighters would pretend they didn't hear the veiled threat, but I could sense their fear more times than not. On the flipside, I must point out there were many firefighters who did an outstanding job in L.A.'s most besieged communities and always behaved respectfully and garnered much admiration from residents. Some became my closest colleagues on and off the job.

I'd have to intervene on behalf of the firemen, too. People in the neighborhood didn't like many firefighters because of that lack of respect, so sometimes they wouldn't give them access to a scene. I had to vouch for the firefighters so the crowd would stand back and let them through. In neighborhoods where people didn't know me, I even got some backlash for being associated with the mostly white firefighters. I'd get stared down walking into a house until somebody recognized me and validated my LTO. "That's Brother Basheer. He's an

O.G. Give him some breathing room. Don't mess with none of them firefighters, they all cool."

Fortunately, L.A.'s Fire Department has changed 180 degrees, although this is not the case in other places, which is why I am drawing attention to the need for understanding and respect. The fire service slowly shifted due to hiring more blacks and Latinos, a new mentality in the leadership, governmental pressure, groups like the Stentorians (African-American firefighters), and a variety of other factors, including my organization, which was called in to train firefighters to become more responsive and respectful to residents.

We also created and implemented a "first responders' street survival 101 training course" to give firefighters a better understanding of street violence and the culture fostering it. To date, more than 1,700 firefighters and paramedics have been trained in hard-core gang and violence intervention. Conversely, fire department leaders instruct my PCITI students in fire-service protocols. Students also visit a fire station and learn how it works. They also learn how to make a formal complaint if the community feels they've been treated disrespectfully.

"It's an unusual model, but it makes sense," says Assistant Chief Kwame Cooper. "We have a better understanding of the socioeconomic conditions in high-risk neighborhoods, and they have a better understanding of how we operate. It's about developing meaningful relationships in the communities we serve."

Knowing how to communicate effectively is the key to effectively handling crime scenes. That knowledge results from understanding the needs of all the different parties that find themselves at the yellow tape, and treating each with calm, respect, and compassion.

4 THE GRAPEVINE: CONTROLLING RUMORS

I was sitting in my car one afternoon and decided to turn on the radio to listen to the news. Within several minutes, I regretted my decision. A shooting had just occurred in front of a middle school. About half a dozen kids were wounded, three critically, including a ten-year-old girl. I knew the shooting was likely gang-related. The school was surrounded by three sets that were longtime, entrenched rivals.

I started calling my contacts in that neighborhood to find out exactly what went down. As I was dialing, the calls flooded in. Although this usually happens when something serious goes down in the hood, this time the calls didn't stop. I knew it had to be real bad. I decided I had better just get to the school. I put the car in drive and jammed it.

The scene was chaos. The school was on lockdown—nobody was allowed in or out, panicked parents huddled beyond the perimeter the fire department had set up, TV trucks were arriving, the squawking noise of police radios was everywhere. I checked my phone. I had four calls from Carmen, a woman who I helped through the murder of her husband a couple years back. Her son and daughter participated in a youth mentoring program I was running at eleven schools then. Something told me to call her first.

Carmen screamed in my ear. "Rosita was shot at the school. She's in surgery, I don't know if she's going to make it. I don't know what to do!"

I got the hospital information from her and told her I would be there as soon as I could. Then one of my team members called. Dinifu helps run the mentoring program at a nearby high school. "Damn bro, shit is bad. This young dude is on the roof of the school building threatening to kill himself. Something 'bout he didn't take care of his sister cus she been shot. He asking for you specifically."

"What's his name?"

"Cristobal. He says he won't move off the roof till he's talked to you." It suddenly hit me—Rosita's older brother.

By the time I got to the high school, the boy had jumped and was being treated for a broken leg and serious internal injuries. He told me he went to pick up Rosita, like he did every day to make sure she got home safely, and found out she had caught the lead spray from an AR-15, a semiautomatic assault rifle. He figured she was dead. Distraught and not knowing what to do, he went back to his school and decided he couldn't live because he had failed to protect his little sister. I called Carmen and found out Rosita was alive, although missing a huge chunk of her right arm.

I was relieved that both children had survived, but I was overcome with sadness that yet another family had been so profoundly affected by violence. I took a couple deep breaths, and then I had to push my feelings aside—I knew there could be more grief-torn families in the aftermath.

I started my calls. News of the events was already traveling through the neighborhood grapevine like a lit fuse. The word was that both the shooting and the roof-jumping had been initiation rites by one of the sets in the area. People were convinced that Rosita had been targeted deliberately and Cristobal was thrown off the roof. Neither story was true, but that's what was being said—and believed—without question. Under gang code at the time, children were off limits. I knew there was going to be payback based on this rumor.

I swung into action, reaching out to a couple of my people who had contact with the major shot callers in the area. Believing both kids had been purposely targeted, the gang leaders were in a rage and already planning retaliation for that same night. We relayed the facts of the situation and told them that both kids had survived. That calmed them down somewhat, but we still had homies who were agitated and wanted to do some damage.

We pressed on the key decision makers that my people and I had gotten our information from personally being on the scenes, and they agreed to stand down for the night. If the youngsters had died, I don't think we could have said anything that could have staved off reprisal. Some homies were still pissed off, though, and my team and I had to keep talking and answering questions for the next couple hours.

Meanwhile, the other set was angry that it was getting blamed for such heinous acts against children and thought the story was just a cover to go after them. They were getting ready to take their own action. I had to get my people to explain the situation to them and get them to back off. After several days of back-and-forth, tempers were defused to the point where we got the rival sets to sit-downs to give each side a clear understanding of what went down. It worked. There was no retaliation over this incident and the family recovered from the tragedy. Rosita is now in college and Cristobal is in the military.

» Controlling Information Flow

Rumor control is a pillar of gang-intervention work. It's probably the task that interventionists are most called on to do, and it's a vital function that directly saves lives. Time and again, incorrect information has resulted in major wars in the hood. Countless lives have been lost because of false assumptions over who was to blame and the failure to verify the so-called facts before retaliation was launched.

A variety of reasons exist for this. Sometimes there's just an honest mistake, but other times people jump to conclusions or are blinded by uncontrolled emotion and cannot see, or don't want to see, the truth. There are also more selfish reasons. Some gang members see opportunities to make names for themselves, or their set, through a reprisal, or they're seeking any excuse to move on an enemy. Sometimes chesslike strategies are played—a finger is wrongly pointed at someone in order to motivate a third party to make a move.

For whatever reason, retaliation is the driver of the cycle of violence that forms the bedrock of gang culture, and rumors play a large role in retaliation. Quashing erroneous information is a priority in containing violence and reestablishing balance in the hood. LAPD Sgt. Curtis Woodle explains: "You can't necessarily stop someone from going out and actually killing, but you can stop the rumors that can lead to them to doing that. That's the stuff you can stop."

In any situation, time is of the essence. Gang members—and others—tend to shoot first and ask questions later. They need to take advantage of the emotion, which typically runs the highest in the immediate aftermath of a killing, in order to pump themselves up to be able to carry out the reprisal.

» Neighborhood Grapevines

In the neighborhoods, "grapevines" are sources of information that are well entrenched due to decades of isolation and a tradition of distrusting official sources that remain hard to counter. News of a shooting, family feud, or street fight runs through the community like a bolt of lightning, especially now that everybody is connected with cell phones. Local residents often hear about these situations before police.

But the grapevine becomes like a game of "telephone" where the truth often gets twisted with each retelling, getting further and further from the facts. Often several stories about a shooting or violent incident will spring up. The problem is that people believe those stories because they come from "personal" sources. Even though that personal source might be a neighbor's cousin's sister-in-law's best friend's son, or just a street dude, they believe that source more than official sources like the news media. Because they are members of the community, interventionists are trusted sources. It is the interventionist's duty to determine the truth and get out the correct information.

As discussed in the previous chapter, the best way to do that is to personally witness the crime scene or at least be on the ground soon after and talk to the people who were there when events transpired. Not only will this give interventionists the basic facts of the incident, their observations will also help them form preliminary conclusions based on their own knowledge of how the street works. This can later be used to assess the truth of stories that are going around. For example, if the victim was hit with one or two bullets, the murder was possibly more a "business" hit. If the body was riddled with gunshots, the killing could have been a personal beef or meant as a threat or a message.

» Network of Contacts

Getting quickly to a crime scene isn't always possible, which is why an interventionist should have a wide range of reliable, trustworthy, and preferably trained contacts in as many neighborhoods as possible. If an interventionist can't get to the scene immediately, they can call a contact to go there and report back.

Once the basic information is obtained, the interventionist needs to validate it to ensure rumors aren't simply being repeated. This is fundamental since our job is to stop false assumptions. Our rule is that information must be checked with two or three sources, at least, preferably including someone who was at the scene.

The way we do this is to have an "investigation response team" that is charged with securing information from the scene. Team members are trained in what questions to ask and have a wide range of contacts based on the respect and relationships they have in the community. A communication tree is essential to quickly identify who is to be called, in what order, and for what reason. Knowing the go-to people within your own organization, and additional people you might need outside your organization, will save time and energy in a crisis.

It is imperative that interventionists keep their mouths sealed about an incident until the facts are checked and double-checked, even if wild rumors are circulating and time is of the essence. Even telling someone who is totally unrelated to the incident can be a fatal mistake. Information moves fast on the street, and it can soon end up hitting the wrong ears and boomeranging back on the interventionists.

I always advise my crew to put the word out on the street that you don't yet have validated information *before* community members and homies start asking what we're hearing. "We're working on it. We have info but we want to make sure it's solid. We'll hit you back when we get it validated" is all you have to say. This helps keep the line of communication flowing with key people in the hood and shows respect to the residents. It also keeps you out front and allows you some control of the situation.

When information is coming at you from all sides, it helps to have a point person, generally a seasoned interventionist, who is in charge of officially updating information and giving the go ahead for releasing it. Likewise, it also helps to have a "war room," a location where incoming information can be assessed and strategic action plans developed in response. This is where you can determine if your communication strategy is working effectively, make adjustments if needed, and later hold a debriefing session to go over the events to see what can be done better next time around.

Once the information is verified, it should first be relayed to key people who you know can be trusted to get the word out without altering it. If possible, relay the information in writing, documented with a date and time, so there is less chance of the recipient getting it wrong. I'm not talking about writing a book here—simple notes jotted on a pad or a one-page outline of events is sufficient.

There will be times when this will be impossible, but this method of passing information is valuable to keep the story straight.

Likewise, keep a list of the people who received the information so you can later authenticate what was put out by you or your team. This not only gives you some control over the flow of your information but lets people know where the information came from. In retelling a story, people usually say where they heard it. Authenticating your information can be necessary because people will often challenge you. They will insist your information is wrong and their version is right. This can be trying at times. Your best defense is being able to backtrack the chain of information from a list of who gave it to whom. It's impossible to track all the people who may have gotten hold of your information, but knowing the last link in the chain can help.

If you do not have any information to pass on, then say that. You don't need to pretend to know it all. It's important not to get caught up in the moment or go on a power trip because everybody is coming up to you and asking questions because they've been told you're in the know. Interventionists must be careful to maintain balance and focus, and remember what the objective is.

》 Correcting Wrong Information

Another aspect of rumor control is dealing with information that's already circulating on the grapevine. Interventionists have to follow this information, determine who put it out and if it's correct. Let me stress that once incorrect intel goes out, it is a daunting task to try to reel it in, even by sending out the correct message.

This is especially true if the information reinforces the desire to seek revenge. If the intel is stoking the emotions of revenge-seekers, it becomes the driving force for how that person or group, or on a larger scale that community, responds. It's a much harder task and requires much more work for the interventionist to correct flawed information as opposed to ensuring correct information is broadcast from the get-go.

I had been called in to stem a wave of street violence in a major city on the East Coast that had resulted in numerous homicides and gunshot wounds. Little did I know it, but I was walking into a nest of ill will on the part of several intervention groups who weren't happy about outsiders coming into their territory.

In the days leading up to the trip, my partners back East called me, asking if I was all right and saying they were worried about me, which I found a little strange. Then another close colleague called me—word was going around on the street out there that L.A. shot callers had put a "green light" on me—I was a target for a hit because of something I had allegedly done. I had to laugh because it was so preposterous, but then I became extremely annoyed. This was the type of rumor that could not only ruin my credibility but also get me and my team killed.

I immediately called my team members and told them to put the word out in L.A. that someone was passing bogus information about me to affiliates on the East Coast. Next, they were to call people and find out who, if anyone, had put this fallacy out in the hood. Third, they were to determine if anybody was upset with me for some reason I wasn't aware of, and lastly the person who was the source of this rumor out East was to be interviewed as to where exactly he got this information. We soon determined what had happened. Individuals from one of the eastern organizations had made a few calls to Los Angeles and had received wrong information. It was another individual who had a similar name to mine who had actually been green lighted. Those folks were so happy to find this out, since they were hoping to tarnish my name and derail my ability to be effective, they did not bother to validate the information, a basic procedure.

An emergency meeting with all the players in the new city collaboration was convened with my people and I conferenced in by phone. The new partners got a chance to dialog with our L.A. folks and have all their concerns addressed. They were satisfied that there was no truth to the rumor, and we proceeded with our work.

The importance of correctly utilizing rumor-control procedure cannot be underestimated. It's a vital tool to control the violence and mayhem that can erupt over simple misinformation.

5 THE WHITE FLAG: NEGOTIATING PEACE

"You want us to come to the table for some damn peace talks? Man, that bullshit is crazy! We respect you, Aquil, but you asking too much. Five of our people are down, three don't look like they coming back. The team been getting jacked for weeks, and everybody wants some serious payback. This shit got to be answered and now, and you want us to *stand down*? Them fools ain't reached out. Matter of fact, word on the street is they wearing this shit with a badge of honor!"

Rawdog, a tough gangster who got his nickname from speaking his mind bluntly, folded his arms and glared at me. His set was in a heavy-duty war with a rival neighborhood led by a respected rival called X, who like Malcolm X had taken the name "X" to represent his unknown African identity.

The tit-for-tat cycle of retaliation between the two sets had been going on for about six months, resulting in seven shootings and the killing of four people, including a seventy-two-year-old lady who was struck by a stray bullet just as she was retiring for the night. The escalating violence had strung a tightrope of tension in the streets. Homeboys set up scout towers to keep tabs on anybody coming into their territories. Mothers were keeping kids indoors, fathers put eyes on any outsiders on their blocks.

It was X who called me, saying something had to be done to defuse the situation before a real bloodbath went down and asking if my team and I could intervene. He knew I had a longstanding relationship with Rawdog—his Pop had been a mentor of mine back in the days of the Black Power movement—and figured if Rawdog would listen to anyone, it would be me. I knew Rawdog respected me, but I also knew it would be a challenge bar none to get him to sit down with his arch enemy and it would take a lot more work to get him to change his mindset. "I'll see what I can do," I told X.

I caught up with Rawdog on the street. His initial rejection of a sit-down was predictable—he saw accepting mediation as a sign of fear and/or weakness. Sighing inwardly, I wiped my brow and then came back at him yet again with the reasons why he should talk peace.

"Real talk, young brother. I know the hood's in pain, but somebody got to take the lead on this. You and I both know if there's not a lid put on this crap, a whole lot more people gonna be in some pain, and that pain gonna be a lot worse than what's going on right now."

Rawdog was having none of it. "You right, there's gonna be a lot more pain to them fools for disrespecting my people and the hood the way they have."

I knew I had to come at this from a different angle if I was going to have any success. I thought quickly. Rawdog had two young children who he loved more than anything. This might be my way in.

"You remember about three years ago, Brother Bull and his family?"

"Man, how could anybody forget that?" Bull's boys, ages five and six, were running to an ice cream truck when they were run over by a pickup truck right in front of the house. One died on the spot, the other lived for two hours. It was an accident caused by reckless driving by the pickup truck driver. It had nothing to do with gang activity.

"You remember what Bull was doing when his two kids died?"

"Yeah, he was working on his ride (car) and the kids got away from him."

"That ain't the whole story. Bull got a call from his people. Their rivals were going to move on the hood because of some mess that went down two days before. Bull was in his garage securing his firepower (guns). While he was in the garage, he saw one of the rivals cruising down the street and make a U-turn to come back by his house. Just then, the ice-cream truck pulled up and the kids burst out the front door calling for him so he could buy them an ice cream. He was crouched behind the car in the garage and never heard them. They ran across the street thinking their daddy was already at the truck. The rest you know."

There was a long silence. I waited, letting the words sink in. Rawdog finally spoke. "Damn, that's some real shit. I wouldn't know what to do if that happened to my kids. Still, Big Bro, that's different than this. Damn, damn." He thought for a moment, rubbed his chin. "Here's the real. I'll talk to my people, see what they think about a mediation, let them know it came through you and you validate it's for real. I don't think it's gonna do no good, but I'll rap with them. I'll reach back out when I got something to say."

"Much respect, Lil Bro." As I walked down the sidewalk, I felt a burst of hope. It was a start.

A couple of weeks passed and there was no word from Rawdog. I had about given up on him when late one night he called. "Look Big Bro, I been putting a lot of thought to the mediation you were talking about. Some of my people ready to sit down, but we ain't gonna meet with them dudes unless you and your people there."

I reassured him we would be. "Gotta ask you a question, young soldier. What changed your mind?" I asked out of curiosity.

"Bro, that story bout Bull stopped me cold. I thought 'bout how his kids ended up losing their lives behind Bull's beef. I don't want mine going out on no humbug like that. Don't get me wrong, homie, I take what happens in my hood seriously, but we gotta give the babies a chance to live."

We moved forward. It took four sit-downs and six private sessions with one side at a time—and a whole lot of cussing, mad-dogging, threatening, foot-stomping, finger-pointing, walking out the room, and throwing up of hands before we were able to iron out a ceasefire. This was one of the good ones. The ceasefire held loosely, little skirmishes back and forth but nothing major. Then something unexpected happened. Rawdog and X's children became friends at school. The two rivals had to tolerate each other for the sake of their kids. Later I found out the hoods privately buried the hatchet. The ceasefire is still in effect today.

» Fragile Work

Conflict and dispute resolution is delicate work that has to be handled with precision. It's one of the most fragile areas in the discipline of professional intervention because the process can break down at any time over a wrong look or misconstrued word, which also creates a lot of stress for the interventionist. Emotions and tempers are running high, especially when deaths have occurred and reputations and respect—the backbone of gang culture—are at stake. Nei-

ther side wants to be perceived as afraid or weak. Nevertheless, conflict resolution is an essential tool in the interventionist's box because it can save countless lives.

In the gang world, conflict-resolution procedures most often come into play to try to end violence. Negotiations usually result in one of three possible outcomes:

* Stand-downs. This is often the first step, a temporary solution that buys time. It can last for just hours. I often use this to get a set bent on avenging a shooting to hold off the retaliation until I find out the facts behind the incident, for instance.

* Ceasefires. This is a longer-term solution with definite time limits and rules. Ceasefires include conditions such as safe zones, like schools and routes to schools, as well as times of day—no shooting before sundown, for example.

* Truces. This is more of a permanent solution where both parties agree to put down their weapons and declare peace. South L.A. gangs agreed to a truce in the wake of the 1992 civil disturbance over the Rodney King verdict. It held strong for a few years.

Interventionists can play three main roles to resolve conflicts: mediators, arbitrators, or facilitators. In all three, the interventionist must do the following groundwork:

 # Define the problem.
 # Identify all parties involved.
 # Obtain permission from the parties to intervene.
 # Possess a respected LTO and the necessary skills to be effective.
 # Be clear on the challenges presented by each side.
 # Be clear on each side's objective, as well as your own.
 # Have several possible solutions to present.
 # Be prepared to construct viable action plans.
 # Be willing to listen.
 # Be flexible.
 # Be ready to be with the engagement for the long term.
 # Monitor the plan once completed.
 # Be ready to call it quits if the dispute can't be resolved.

» Mediation

Mediation is the most commonly used form of conflict resolution. There are two types of mediation in violence intervention work: regular mediation and street mediation. The first deals with any type of conflict that may arise—including personal beefs and domestic-violence issues—while the second deals directly with gang and street violence. The stakes in street mediation are usually higher because if a solution is not figured out, there is a strong possibility of loss of life. In these cases, pressure and stress can be high on the mediator.

The basic goals for any mediation are to:

 # Intervene to help the two sides reach an agreement that resolves the dispute.
 # Assist the sides to bring about an improved communication process.

It is vital that mediators be fair to all parties involved and do not judge. Your role is to act as a guide and get the parties to a point where they make their own decisions and hopefully come up with a workable solution.

The basic guidelines for mediators are to:

Listen.

Be neutral and impartial.

Suggest, do not dictate.

Let the disputing parties determine the conditions of a settlement.

Arbitration

Arbitration is used when stalemates occur. Both sides feel their requests are fair but the other side is being inflexible. An arbitrator can be brought in as an impartial judge to resolve the difference and impose a solution. The arbitrator is usually known and trusted by both parties, who agree to submit to the arbitrator's final decision.

Crown Park had been taken over by a gang that started charging a "tax" to anyone who used the playground or playing fields, as well as simply beating down people they didn't like who entered the park. Flooded with complaints, the local city council representative got police to step up patrols, but that failed to get the gang out. The city turned to a local nonprofit, who in turn subcontracted a trusted gang-intervention agency to help. All was good until they got down to hazard pay for the interventionists. The organizations went back and forth for weeks over the amount, meanwhile the park situation was getting worse. Finally, I was called in to arbitrate and come up with an equitable solution. Both sides agreed to accept my judgment. After three days of talks, I came up with an agreement—the pay was adjusted and the nonprofit obtained more say in the process with the interventionists. The interventionists went to work, eventually returning the park to neighborhood children.

Facilitation

Facilitation usually occurs when disagreeing parties are close to reaching common ground but just can't get to the end point. Facilitators can come in and provide points of clarity without adding content to the process. At the same time, they assist the parties to bring forth their best thinking capability, create sustainable harmony, and, once agreements are made, maintain them. This often comes into play at the end of a dispute resolution when serious issues and challenges have been worked through and the parties are attempting to create the best end product but are having difficulty in achieving that goal.

The Process

Mediators must have almost unlimited patience. It can take countless hours of going back and forth between the parties just to get them to agree to sit down at a table across from one another. It can involve meetings at all hours of the day and night, and there are often sudden setbacks such as changing of minds about a sit-down. Mediators must remain cool in the face of emotionalism and big egos.

Once you get both sides to agree to a mediation, the first task is setting up the ground rules, which is basically a mediation in itself. A neutral location to hold the talks must be found and approved by both sides. A basic requirement is that it be located on impartial turf. I often use my headquarters, which is a known neutral zone. Maintaining neutrality is essential to developing trust to go into the process and keeping it throughout.

The list of attendees must be vetted and okayed by both sides. Both parties will usually insist on having an equal number of their crew attend. They must also be equal in stature within their own hierarchies. Sending underlings to talk with a shot caller can be viewed by the shot caller as an insult and derail the process from the start. The mediator should insist on a no weapons rule, and parties must agree to be searched.

At the session, the mediator will give a brief statement of purpose and go over the rules—no physical aggression, only one person speaks at a time, each side will speak in turn. Then the mediator should let the parties talk, only stepping in to enforce rules or quiet things down if tempers get heated. The biggest mistake that mediators make is to try and control the process. That should be left to the parties.

Although mediators should have a high level of respect from both sides, their credibility is going to be questioned throughout the process. An interventionist who was affiliated with one neighborhood may be perceived as being partial to that hood, for example. Some might even perceive the interventionist as being part of the problem. The mediator must be able to read the temperatures of all involved and bend when the situation dictates. Being ready for emotional blow-ups and verbal thrashing is part of the game. You cannot take the process personally.

Individuals who do mediations must be trained and experienced because of its tricky nature. I always recommend interventionists intern with media-

tion practitioners before attempting to go it alone. This is easier said than done. Most serious mediations are closed, and mediators are in that position because they have solid credibility and validated LTOs with the parties. A newcomer to the circle is not looked upon lightly. This can sometimes be overcome when it's explained to the groups that the newcomer will ride on the mediator's validation and that the mediator will take full responsibility should anything go awry. The decision to allow the newcomer to attend is usually dictated by how much standing the mediator has with the groups.

Breakdowns

Interventionists must be prepared for mediation breakdowns. These are disheartening because simply getting rivals to a sit-down is a feat in itself, requiring a lot of time and energy. Talks can go awry for many reasons—too much entrenched hatred between the parties, homies not really committed to a mediation, dislike for particular individuals at the table, the desire for revenge, the failure to offer atonement for past acts, or the failure to agree on terms. There's no answer other than to start the process all over.

Your first consideration is to let some time elapse. Tempers run high and emotions are fragile when talks collapse. Often times, the failure heightens the rivalry and the situation actually becomes worse. Once some time passes and you have some assurance that temperaments are edging back to normal, the interventionist should try and restart the process. This is only if the disagreements weren't so great that you feel it is possible to achieve some degree of success. All parties have to be willing to come back to the table. Typically you have to do much more lobbying because you now have to create additional reasons why they should come back to the table when it didn't work before. Many times these reasons will sadly involve a fresh spate of violence—more homicides or injuries, or a police crackdown.

Pulling the Plug

Lastly, the interventionist has to recognize when mediation is just not going to work. After several sessions, if the parties refuse to budge from their positions and there's no spirit of cooperation or the will to come to terms, you have to pull the plug. If this happens, you have to attempt to get the parties to at least leave the table in a better position than when they came in, such as agreeing to check the facts of an incident before retaliating. At the very least you want them to remain at an equal position. You don't want them returning to the street with more animosity than when they came in. You also want to stress that you will be available if anyone would like to restart the process.

Follow-Up

An important aspect of mediation is the follow-up. Once you leave the table with an agreement in hand, compliance must be monitored. The interventionist must check in constantly with the parties to ensure the sides are keeping to their ends of the bargain. This is easier said than done. The parties often don't want to be bothered by what they consider already done and over with, and don't like feeling you're checking up on them. You have to remember there are no written obligations here and no one owes you anything. You were a guest brought into the process because of your LTO and reputation. Nevertheless, follow-up still must be done. If adjustments are needed, you must bring individuals back to the table.

Conflict resolution is one of the most time- and energy-consuming components of intervention work. It is a process fraught with the risk of failure, but the potential reward is great—an end to violence.

6 THE VICTIMS: DEALING WITH THE GRIEVING

I had known Julie for many years. In her younger days she had skated on the edge of gang life, largely through a boyfriend who was in it. But as she matured, she left all that behind, got married to another guy, and was focused on raising their two small children. Then that old boyfriend resurfaced. He had never accepted the fact that Julie had left him. He used to say that she belonged to him and would always. After going along with that for years, Julie finally packed up and left. She didn't see him again until he re-entered her life with a vengeance.

In a fit of jealousy-driven revenge, he murdered her husband and six-year-old daughter, strangling them as well as torturing the husband. Julie had seen the horrific display of their bodies in their home before she called me, sobbing. I stayed with her for hours at the scene, later taking her for coffee so she could collect her thoughts. She often stared blankly as we talked and made a plan for her to stay with her sister.

Following interventionist protocol to assist victims, I kept her company until the sister arrived and promised to follow up with her the next day, confident that she seemed as stable as she could be under the circumstances. (I'll relate the rest of the story later in the chapter.)

One of the toughest parts of the interventionist's job is seeing the victim's family at the most painful point of loss, usually either at the crime scene or the hospital. This is where they may first learn of their loved one's premature death, bear the full frontal assault of viewing a bullet-torn body, or witness the relative's last breath.

Sometimes it may not be a death but a catastrophic injury that can leave family members struggling to grapple with the prospect of giving lifetime care. The expression of anguish and agony can be overwhelming. In my opinion, this is what takes an emotional toll on the interventionist more than the actual violence.

» Keeping Emotional Distance

To do our work, interventionists must be empathetic but also keep an emotional distance, although doing so can be extremely difficult. Interventionists can't help but feel with the family, picture their own loved one lying there. Countless times I have had to hold back my emotions when dealing with victims' families, but pushing feelings aside and staying neutral is essential in order to get the work done.

The first thing an interventionist must do is remove the family members from the immediate crime scene and away from the sight of their loved one. Taking them to a quiet place down the block or seating them in a car gets them far enough away from the source of stress to re-establish a sense of normality. Often times they are in denial that their family member is dead and want to see the body, or if the victim is alive, they will naturally want to go to him or her. But this will interfere with the crime scene, which needs to be preserved for the investigation.

Remaining at the actual scene can wreak havoc on the family, who want to relive the sequence of events, blame themselves for the tragedy, or attempt to believe it never happened and the victim is still alive. There may also be angry homeboys talking up reprisal that can add to the stress.

A good interventionist will take family members aside, explaining sympathetically that police and paramedics have to do their job, and call in an interventionist who is a victim-engagement specialist if one isn't already there or perform that function themselves. Victim-engagement interventionists are specially trained in "mental-health first aid" and crisis and stress management. Often our domestic-violence counselors take on this responsibility.

I created this specialization after seeing at numerous crime scenes that distraught relatives were left for the most part unattended. Other family members, friends, and neighbors were often scared to walk into the scene of the shooting or stabbing, and sometimes survivors felt that professional psychologists and counselors were too detached and they couldn't establish a rapport with them.

» Victim Engagement

The goal of the victim-engagement interventionist is to bring a level of functioning normality to the survivors by taking care of their immediate needs. They may need a safe location to stay if the home has been shot up or there's the potential for further violence. They may need childcare or transportation if they have to go to the hospital. Other relatives have to be contacted. They will need to eat, although they rarely do. They may need simply to vent, and the interventionist must sit, listen, and express calm support to establish a relationship.

While talking to them, the interventionists should also be on the lookout for talk of retaliation and drug or alcohol use that may be heightening the survivors' emotions, as well as suicidal signs. Training in how to talk to survivors is important. At first, because they're in shock, victims may not take in everything that's being said to them. Interventionists must be patient and prepared to repeat things numerous times until the person understands.

The interventionist also must tell the victims what is going to happen procedurally—the coroner will take the body to the morgue, for example—so they are prepared. Later, because of their fragile emotional state and the loss that has cast them adrift, family members look to interventionists for advice. They tend to key in on every word you say. You must focus on what is best for the victim and make sure any promises made are kept.

Victim-engagement work does not end at the crime scene or hospital. You've got to be there for the duration, and that could be months. Interventionists should check in with the families to ensure they are stabilized and offer help with practical issues. This can run the gamut from funeral arrangements to social-service aid. Interventionists must be prepared with all kinds of resources and ensure they have a network of reliable go-to people such as mental-health counselors.

The nineteen-year-old son of a friend of mine had been killed in a spray of gunfire from a drive-by shooting in a neighboring city. The four gang members who were in the car were quickly arrested and eventually went on trial for murder. My friend Ibrahim attended the trial but had to run a gauntlet of the defendants' homeboys every day he went to court. They followed him in the parking lot, threatened him in the elevator, stared him down in the courtroom. They also heckled witnesses and prosecutors.

I went with Ibrahim to court several times to give him moral support, but I couldn't make it to every day of the weeks-long trial. I knew he needed formidable help—he was already dealing with the emotional devastation caused by his son's murder and now he had to deal with the psychological trauma of the terrorization by his supposed murderers. So I called in some victim-services interventionists to accompany him. They not only assisted him in court, they also helped him with basic family functions.

Veteran L.A. interventionist Blinky Rodriguez had to call a congressman's office for the relatives of a sixteen-year-old who was killed in a gang-related drive-by as he rode a bicycle down the street. The boys' grandparents were in Mexico and wanted to attend the funeral, but they were turned back at the border because they lacked visas to enter the United States. Blinky got help from a local congressman to get them through so they could say goodbye to their grandson at the funeral, which was held in his parents' living room. Blinky also got a $6,000 cemetery plot donated to the family. "We help families who don't know how they're going to bury their sons," Blinky says.

» Hospitals

Steve was a young father of three who was trying to leave the gang life after many years. Problem was he had been good at what he did—he had made a lot of enemies. On his way home from work one evening, Steve was shot by a passing car on the freeway. His wife called me in a panic—Steve was alive, but he had spotted a rival's car following the ambulance. There was only one reason for that—they meant to finish the job.

I knew paramedics would be taking him to the closest trauma center, not the nearest hospital ER, and I headed straight there, arriving before the ambulance. My team informed the sheriff's deputies posted there of a possible shooting in the making. They called in extra deputies and stationed them around the ER area and alerted hospital staff, who took measures to restrict ER access and be on the lookout. Steve was transported into the ER safely. While he was undergoing surgery, the rivals circled the hospital several times to make their point of being seen and their presence felt. They eventually left.

Hospitals can be prime locations for retaliation moves, bids to "finish the job" by killing the wounded, and scenes of high emotional drama. But medical centers are often underprepared when they come up against gang culture.

Adversaries have been known to follow ambulances, or, if they can find out where the victim is being transported to, they'll be waiting for the ambulance to pull up and the gurney to roll out. Gang members are all-too familiar with the layouts and procedures at hospitals. Emergency rooms usually have little security, and homeboys can easily enter, saying they're the victim's family. There have been instances of victims being blasted while lying on a gurney in the ER or, more often, physical assaults where the victim ends up on the floor.

Interventionists can be of vital use at hospitals that see a lot of violent crime victims. A few hospitals in Los Angeles have their own interventionists who are called to the ER when paramedics radio in that a gang-related shooting victim is en route. But most don't. If they feel there could be a possibility of a move at the hospital, interventionists at the crime scene should try to find out where the victim is being transported and get to the medical center before the paramedics do to act as a buffer. Interventionists can talk down rival adversaries as well as help the family. If the interventionists can't get there quickly, they should call colleagues nearer the trauma center.

Sometimes fights can break out between rivals who encounter each other at a hospital over completely unrelated matters or when one of their own homeboys or relatives is the victim. Pete's sister had been badly beaten by a boyfriend, and she was rushed to the local emergency room. When Pete, a respected O.G., arrived at the hospital with four homies, he saw his bruised and bloodied sister lying barely conscious on a gurney pushed against the wall. "Where's the goddamn doctor?" he yelled. Hospital staff, who had worked with my intervention team many times before, called us right away.

A nurse tried to quiet Pete, but he brushed her off and grabbed the first white coat he saw. "Why the hell my sister ain't been taken care of? I'm gonna blow the roof off this damn slaughter house if she ain't looked at right now!"

"Sir, we will take care of her when we can. There are other patients with…"

"Fuck that, you ain't heard what I just said, idiot!"

Two of my team members rushed in and started trying to talk him down. "Pete, they got procedures they got to follow, man, let them do their work. They gonna take care of her," the interventionist said.

Pete's eyes were wild with fury and pain. "They better get their asses in gear. I'm about to light this damn place up!"

One of the interventionists spoke to the staff. The sister was taken to a private room and evaluated, which the staff was going to do anyway, but at our suggestion, they altered the procedure so Pete could witness something being done. He calmed down. The interventionists took him outside and stayed with him until his sister was treated.

» Candelight Vigils

Victims' families, or sometimes their homeboys, often want to hold a memorial for their loved one with a candlelight vigil. These events can be important outlets to relieve stress and grief, but they can also be venues for moves by rival gangs. Not only are they large gatherings but also people's guards are down. The very structure of a vigil—a circle facing inward with backs toward the street—presents a prime target for those seeking revenge.

Trained interventionists can prevent further tragedy from happening by taking precautionary measures depending on the potential for retaliation. One is having the crowd meet in a central location and then drive together to the place of the vigil so people cannot be attacked while walking to the vigil location. The victim's family and all children should be placed at the core of the circle. Lookouts should be posted at access points around the vigil location, which should always have several exit routes in case chaos breaks out.

A key factor to watch out for is drug and alcohol use by grievers. Homeboys can use a candlelight vigil as a time to get together to psych themselves up to go out and do some damage. Interventionists can try and talk down the firebrands by saying that it would be a disrespect to the family and to the victim. Another cautionary measure is to keep the event structured so people don't hang around all night getting loaded, then go out to seek revenge. For example, the vigil will start at 7:00 PM, the prayer said at 7:10, the joining of hands at 7:15, remembrances at 7:20, with the conclusion at 7:45.

» Funerals

Eduardo was kicking back with a buddy on the street in Pasadena one afternoon when a guy walked up to him, took out a gun, and squeezed the trigger. It was a fatal wound. Eduardo died at age nineteen. Distraught and angered by the senseless killing, his family blamed Eduardo's friends, saying that their gangbanging had caused the murder. Eduardo had not even been a gang member. The homeboys were also grief-stricken. In gang tradition, they held several car washes to raise money to pay for the victim's funeral and help his family. They earned more than $2,000, but Eduardo's family refused to accept the cash. Not only that, the family told them they could not attend the viewing and burial. The friends were devastated.

Yvette McDowell, a former paramedic and Pasadena city prosecutor who is now a PCITI-trained interventionist, was called in to help. "I spent a lot of time on the phone with the older brother, who was kind of speaking for the family. He was adamant that the friends not come to the viewing. I tried to tell him they felt really bad. They wanted the money to go to his family and his memory. I asked him to let them grieve in their own way. He was their friend. They felt a kinship, a sense of family with him."

After many conversations, the brother finally relented, accepting the money and allowing three friends to attend the viewing at the cemetery only if they were escorted by the interventionists. "I drove them down, waited till there was some distraction, ushered them in and out, and drove them back," Yvette recalls. "They wanted to be able to pay their respects. That meant the world to them."

As mentioned in Chapter 2, funerals are an important part of gang culture. Paying last respects is a way of validating the premature end to a young life, of making sure it was not in vain. But like candlelight vigils, funerals can be ideal targets for retaliation and sometimes even spark wars. We have had incidents in Los Angeles where rival gang members have created chaos at funerals, overturning caskets and even removing bodies. There are ways to prevent this.

Interventionists must first check the location of the funeral and the route that mourners will take from there to the cemetery to determine if these fall in turf controlled by different gang sets, particularly neighborhoods that are adversaries to the victim's set. If so, contact must be made with local shot callers to obtain a stand-down, akin to a pass, for the duration of the funeral. As we saw in Chapter 2, that doesn't always happen. If that permission is not obtained, it can be taken as a sign of blatant disrespect and incite violence. Funeral routes sometimes may have to go a mile or two out of their way to avoid areas of potential difficulty.

Sometimes two funerals are held: one for family and friends and another for homeboys. As in the case cited above, homies can take offense if they are not allowed at a funeral. In either case, security measures should be taken. These include posting sentries inside and outside the church or funeral venue, as well as people at the door checking for infiltrators among the mourners, looking out for bulky clothing that could be concealing a weapon, for example. Law-enforcement sources can also be tapped to act as visual physical deterrents. Officers in squad cars can sit outside the venue or pass by on frequent patrols.

I always recommend that interventionists establish relationships with local clergy to alert them about gang funerals and advise them on security measures. Sometimes pastors may have their own security, but often they do not. Likewise, when negotiating cease-fires, I always urge that houses of worship be earmarked as off-limits for gang activity, but that cannot always be achieved. Funeral security is a vital part of intervention.

» Moving Forward

When the doorbell rang at 6:30 one morning, Stinson Brown knew something was off. He opened the door to find homicide detectives with faces somber as stone. His twenty-one-year-old son, a college student and football player, had been shot to death at a party shortly before midnight. A seventeen-year-old gang member was later arrested for the murder. Sitting through the trial two years later, Stinson learned the teenager had killed his son because he saw him talking to girls.

"The only thing I can think of is jealousy. My son was clean-cut, six-foot three, 240 pounds; the young man was somewhat short in stature. My son had left the party and then returned to pick up two young ladies like the gentleman he was raised to be. He was standing by the car when the young man walked up to him and shot him without provocation. The young man said at the trial he had never spoken to my son."

I've known Stinson for many years. He's an officer with the LAPD—off-duty, he runs an outstanding mentoring program called Brother II Brother, which has helped hundreds of young men find their footing in life. At the time of his son's murder, he was working as a drill instructor at the police academy. He's now a gang-intervention liaison officer in South L.A. With what he went through, it wasn't easy for him to switch to a job in the criminal gang homicide unit, but

after months of soul-searching he decided to do it as part of his life's calling. "I embrace my role as an opportunity to make a difference. Someone may hear what I have to say: There is no reason why we should be losing human life at this rate in this country," he says.

The emotional triggers that he knew the job would present are there, but he's found ways of coping. At the scene of a double homicide, the sight of a sixteen-year-old's face before the coroner zipped up the body bag was a vivid and painfully sharp reminder of his own loss and the fact that he'll never get over it. He shared his personal story with the victim's mother and then went home to regroup emotionally.

"I watch Westerns on TV with a glass of lemonade and shut down. That's what I have to do. I had to let the hatred and bitterness go because it was too much for me to carry. You can rise above retaliation. I forgave the young man in open court. At the trial, I began to understand things in his childhood that shaped his behavior. I pray that during his incarceration he can come to grips with what he did."

I don't know of any victim who has been able to fully recover from the premature loss of a loved one through an act of violence. It changes your life forever.

Some, like Stinson, have found a way to make sense out of a senseless act by committing the rest of their own lives to preventing violence.

Blinky Rodriguez was already working informally with youth in the martial arts when his sixteen-year-old son was fatally shot in a gang drive-by as he sat in a car in front of a high school in 1992. Blinky and his late wife, Lilly, decided to embark on a mission to save other kids from the same fate. Blinky is now a well-known force in the northeast San Fernando Valley outside of Los Angeles, working with some seventy-five Latino gangs. His son's death, he says, was "the deep, deep line of demarcation. There was a conscientious decision. I chose to fight for the lives of people."

Turning Personal

Thirty years ago I lost one of my two brothers to street violence. My family was devastated—I was really knocked to the ground. I had always played the role of family protector, and I was overcome with guilt that I hadn't been there for him. I was already heavily involved in intervention work, but at his funeral, I pledged to make hard-core violence intervention my primary mission as a way of ensuring his life had not been in vain. Thereafter, whenever I felt burnt out by the work, discouraged to the point of quitting, I remembered my vow to my brother and found the strength to keep going.

The police never found his killers. For two years I hunted them myself, taking risks I never should've taken, endangering my life on several occasions. I'm glad I didn't find them—I wouldn't be walking these streets freely today. Instead, I channeled my anger and grief into resolve and commitment, and found true empathy for victims' families because I had been there, too. His death made violence eradication a very personal goal for me; it served to crystallize my life's purpose.

Tragic Aftermath

Sadly, some victims are irretrievably broken by their experience of loss. The story I started this chapter with does not have a happy ending, but I tell it to show that the aftermath of violence can be just as tragic as the initial act.

After leaving Julie in the care of her sister, I was awakened by a frantic call around 5:00 AM. The sister told me Julie had fed her five- year old son an overdose of pills and then OD'd herself, during the night. They were both dead.

In a suicide note, Julie wrote that she was so overwhelmed with what she saw and the prospect of the difficult aftermath that lay ahead, that she had decided to commit suicide and take her son's life midway through our conversation the night before. I was shocked and numb. Questions ran in an endless loop through my mind as I felt the burden of guilt and responsibility settle on my shoulders. Did I have ownership in the suicide? Could I have prevented it by saying or doing something different? Should I have seen this coming?

I know these questions are unanswerable, and I cannot afford to linger on them. If I do, they will cloud my ability to handle future situations. Still, I also know the questions and the search for answers will stay with me forever. In the meantime, I use them as a motivation to continue my work.

Working with victims is the most emotionally draining part of working the streets, but it's essential to a healthy healing process. When victims feel supported and cared for, they are less likely to seek revenge on others or engage in self-destructive habits such as drugs and alcohol. That makes for a healthier community on the whole.

7 THROWDOWNS AND SHOWDOWNS

One of PCITI's banner community programs is our "Feed the Need" food give-away that we do at least quarterly in low-income neighborhoods, as well as a holiday giveaway that provides families with Thanksgiving turkeys and trim-mings as well as Christmas toys. The items are donated by a businessman–phi-lanthropist we have a close relationship with, Mark Chow, who heads A Founda-tion for Kids. We hold the events at local parks, and since they draw big crowds, we take the opportunity to promote peace and do some community mobiliza-tion as well.

The events normally run smoothly, but one time a loud squabble erupted among a dozen people. Some local residents objected to two families associ-ated with a rival neighborhood coming to get "their" food. I dispatched a couple interventionists to defuse the altercation, and we provided food for the other families. We assumed the situation was over. But ten minutes later, five cars pulled up with screeching tires and blocked the street where the food truck was parked. About twenty gang members from the adjacent hood jumped out.

"Nobody gets no damn food unless our people are taken care of, or we'll shut all this shit down!" one of the shot callers hollered.

About fifteen homies from the local hood immediately rolled up. "Bullshit, who the hell are you? It ain't going down like that," one said.

The two sides glared at each other while people standing in the line, mostly women and young children, grew visibly nervous. I jumped off the truck and went to see what I could do. I called over two main players from the rival neighborhood and got two shot callers from the local hood. They agreed to an emergency meeting, and we moved to a back area of the park.

I explained there was only enough food for certain number of people that day, but if we could resolve this issue peacefully, I would commit to bringing a truckload of groceries to the other community the next weekend. Furthermore, if we had any food left from the current giveaway, we would let the other community have access to it. Lastly, we agreed to do a joint neighborhood day where we would give away clothing in addition to groceries.

The opposing hood agreed with reservations. "We'll back off, but you homeboys better keep your word." The crisis was resolved. Dialogue aborted what could have blown up into a violent situation with numerous innocent casualties, but more importantly we offered options and resources, and kept our promises. Eventually, we were able to pull those two communities together.

Street-crisis management is another important component of disrupting violence. Street crises are violent situations that can erupt at any moment. Some are spillovers from gang beefs, but most are not. They're often fights, with fists or weapons, that break out at parties or on corners. They're frequently fuelled by drugs and alcohol—people who are high or looking to get high—or sometimes just by desperation that drives someone to a breaking point. These tend to be volatile situations, and a key part of intervention here is taking measures to ensure that interventionists do not endanger themselves.

» Preparing to Intervene

The first step is assessing the crisis. It's useful to use the 4W&H risk formula I created a decade ago:

Ask yourself who, what, when, why, and how questions as each word relates to the situation at hand. For example, relevant questions to ask might be: Do you know who the threat is? Do you know what is causing the problem? When did it occur? Why is this happening? How is it going down? A "yes" answer to each question is awarded 20 percent. Once all questions have been answered, the total percentage will give you your chance of success and survival in the encounter. It's advisable to have at least a 60 percent chance before going in.

Interventionists do not have to engage in every situation they come across. In fact, they shouldn't get involved until first considering the risk of danger to themselves. In street situations where violence is the norm, the risks need to be clearly identified. "Risk factors" include whether people are verbally arguing or throwing fists, if there's a weapon, if they are sober or intoxicated. But there are also "risk triggers," the catalysts that escalate the threat to a crisis.

Two hood leaders are beefing in the street—that's a risk factor. Then more crew members arrive. The potential for a violent showdown has just risen substantially. They are risk triggers. One lifts his shirt to show a gun in his waistband—an immediate risk trigger. When a risk trigger appears, the key is to determine what would prevent the trigger from going off. If you can figure out what is going to cause the explosion, you should be able to either defuse the explosion or at least minimize its impact. The risk of impact to you and the kind of impact, as in the possibility of getting shot, should determine the level of your commitment.

A Tragedy Stemming from Assumptions

Gerald had been doing intervention work for over a decade and had a true talent for mediating crisis. He and his wife went one night to a neighborhood function at a social hall, and an argument between two middle-aged gentlemen, Ron and Sam, broke out near the refreshment table. They both had had too much to drink, and Sam accused Ron of disrespecting his wife. Although the wife tried to convince Sam that hadn't been the case, he didn't believe it.

Sam was escorted to his car and asked to stay there until his wife came. Instead, Sam got his gun from the car and returned to the party, where he confronted Ron. Thinking the confrontation was more bravado than anything else, Gerald approached the men with the goal of retrieving the gun and taking Sam home. Ron seized the distraction to wrest the gun away from Sam. A scuffle broke out and two shots were fired, striking Gerald in the neck and head. He died on the spot.

Gerald's biggest mistake was miscalculating the risk, because he allowed assumptions about the two men, not their behavior, to dictate his course of action. Because Sam was brandishing a deadly weapon, Gerald should have assumed the worst—Sam was not playing; he wanted to wound or kill. Gerald should also have considered that emotionalism was driving Sam's actions and that alcohol was involved. Both those factors meant that Sam was not operating from a base of rational thought. If, after considering all that, Gerald still decided to intervene, he should have approached Sam using the bar or the table as cover.

Another mistake Gerald made was viewing Sam as the only threat. Although Sam posed the greater threat with the gun, Ron was also riled up and drunk. Both men were potential dangers. Gerald needed to secure help from other men at the gathering to isolate both of them. In the end, it was the actions of Ron, the lesser threat, that actually cost Gerald his life.

If you intervene, you need to develop a situation-specific plan of action using procedures that you have learned thoroughly beforehand. It's vital that you do not assume the encounter is like something you've handled in the past. Every engagement is different and has its own risks. Looking at it like the "same old same old" will restrict your judgment and handicap your response.

Make sure you have enough people to carry out the intervention plan and that each knows their responsibilities. You should also have a contingency plan in case things go awry. It is much better to scale down what you have to do, as opposed to scaling up because you weren't prepared.

Before heading to the scene, you should tell an off-scene, trustworthy contact your estimated time of arrival, time of departure, and the location of the engagement. Make sure you know exactly where you're going. This is basic information and yet the thing most people forget first. You must know where you are if you need to summon help. Your backup cannot waste valuable time trying to find you.

Keep the contact apprised of your progress when you can during the engagement, and when it is over, let them know you're safe. If there has been no contact within the stated time period, the contact person should assume the engagement went bad and summon assistance.

Managing the Crisis

As you approach the engagement, you should utilize what I call the S.T.O.P. formula—Slow down, Think, Observe, Plan. Once you have the plan, walk head-on toward the individuals. This allows you to view the subjects in advance, possibly identifying any risk triggers and red-flag behaviors. If the subjects are brandishing weapons, move from cover to cover as you approach. Objects made of metal or cement make ideal covers—a car's engine block, a mailbox, a lamppost, a wall, a trash bin. Identify cover ahead of time in case you need it during the encounter.

Nearing the scene, it's important to take stock of your physical surroundings. The key here is locating exits and places to protect yourself. Ensure you have more than one exit point in case one is blocked. Avoid dead ends, street endings, and building layouts that could lock you into an area easily controlled by others. Prevent surprise approaches by locating a wall you could use to place your back to, and check for cover or crevices where individuals could be hiding. Lastly, pinpoint a place you could take refuge in if the situation goes bad and you have no time to leave.

When you arrive at the scene, stay on the perimeter of the confrontation. This allows you to view the entire event, move around easily to gain a 360-degree perspective, and keeps you from being surrounded. Your stance is also important. Stand with one foot forward, one foot back. This effectively cuts your body mass in half, giving the adversary a smaller target. It also puts your body on a firmer foundation, as opposed to standing with feet together, in case of a physical attack.

Isolate the threatening person by encircling him with your team members. In a neutral tone, ask what his issues of concern are, what he specifically wants to resolve the problem, and if there are any other options he would accept if his main demand cannot be met. While talking, keep a watch on his hands and eyes. People usually hit with a hand or hold a weapon in a hand. If you can see the hands, you usually have a chance to prepare for the blow. Likewise, you can be ready by monitoring eye movements. The eyes signal which part of the body will move and in what direction.

You should quickly assess the person's physical appearance—if he looks intoxicated, for example—but more importantly, you should focus intensely on the individual's actions. Certain behaviors reveal aggressive people's intent: invading your personal space, encircling you or boxing you in, blocking your exit, distracting your attention, antagonizing you, distorting your logical thinking process, isolating you, identifying and getting you to acknowledge your weaknesses, continually asking questions for you to answer, signaling that they are in control.

These gestures do not necessarily include aggressive language. In fact, what the person says may be quite innocent. For example, a person asks you for the time, but he slowly keeps approaching you—he is violating your personal space. If someone says he's not looking for a problem but stands in your way, he's blocking your exit or boxing you in. If you say "no," but she keeps talking, telling you that you don't mean what you say, she is distorting your rational thinking.

Focusing on words—not actions—is what trips up a lot of interventionists. They think they're making headway because of what people are saying. If someone is intent on doing damage, he'll chump you with words until he gets to the level of violence he is looking for. The bottom line: The old saying, "it's not what they say, it's what they do," should be followed to the letter.

Keep an adequate response zone around you—the area in which you feel mentally and physically comfortable to respond to a threat (see the example in the figure below). This will be a different space for every individual, determined by training, experience, capability, and factors in the immediate moment, but a good rule of thumb is to stay out of the threat's arm's reach—about two feet—to avoid getting hit, grabbed, or stabbed.

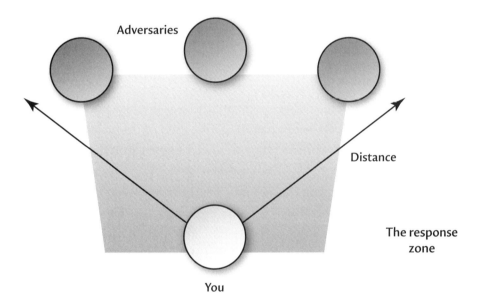

You must always stay aware and try to control your location in regard to the hazard. A person intent on doing harm will start by closing in on you. If you let them get too close, you can't exit the scene or defend yourself because you don't have the space or time to get out of the way.

Lastly, you should continually assess your progress and check that you're using the right procedure as circumstances develop. You must be ready to make adjustments, revert to the backup plan, change the entire course of action, or stand down, if necessary.

I was hanging out on the street one night with two groups of youngsters I knew well. They were drinking "short dogs"—wine coolers—and as often happens when alcohol is involved, words started flying. Small talk at first, which escalated into seemingly fun threats, but then it got physical. Some of the guys pulled out bumperjacks, and it was obvious it was going down. I tried to calm it down, and in doing so, I turned slightly so part of my back was facing one of the guys. I felt something sharp. I wheeled around and saw one of the fools had a blade. I took him to the ground and disarmed him.

It wasn't until later that I discovered a seven-inch laceration on my back. I learned a serious lesson about response zones from that incident. I positioned myself too close to an assailant and turned my back on him. My other mistakes were getting involved in a situation with a high risk factor due to alcohol and assuming that since both sides were friends of mine, I wouldn't be a mark. In sum, I had given them the opportunity to see me as a potential target.

» Keeping Cool

A friend of mine had enlisted in the Army and was giving a going away party at his house. I wasn't big on house parties. Some kind of drama always seemed to go down at them, but I went to this one since I knew I wouldn't be seeing Tom for a year or two.

I arrived early and planned to hightail it early, before everyone got too loaded and the madness started. It was already crowded—people had spilled out of the two-car garage where the party was located and down the driveway. As I elbowed my way through, I felt uneasy, though I couldn't pinpoint exactly why. I decided to stay just a short while.

Midway through the evening, screams slashed through the music. A huge man, over six-feet tall and weighing three hundred pounds, had parked his bear-like bulk in front of the side door with a smirk on his face and an automatic pistol in his hand. He stretched out his arm and calmly started firing at people, his arm moving side to side like a wind-up toy. People dropped to the floor, diving behind couches and the bar for cover.

I was standing about five feet from the guy—whose name I later found out was John—on his right side. He turned, and we were suddenly eye-to-eye, his gun directly pointed at my face. I froze, staring back at him. After a couple seconds that passed like an eternity, John finally spoke. "What the fuck you looking at fool? You like what you see? You want some of this? I should blast your ass just like all these other punks up in here."

I stayed still as a statue. I didn't know why he was talking to me instead of shooting, and I knew I had to seriously weigh my response. What if I said the "wrong" thing that would cause his finger to squeeze that trigger?

"You ain't got no voice, punk?"

I answered in a firm voice with the first thing that came to my mind. "Don't want none, won't be none."

He looked at me. "Get your punk ass outta my face!" He turned and got off a few more rounds. I seized the opportunity to duck behind him and speed out of that garage. Outside, I found one of John's homies had been assaulting people with a small lead pipe.

The tally was three people dead, five wounded—one was paralyzed. I found out that John and his set had shot up the party to make a name for themselves, to gain power by invoking fear. That's why they didn't bother hiding their faces.

The lesson of the incident: It's essential to remain cool, disciplined, and think logically in a crisis. Keep frustration and anger in check. Don't take anything personally—a clear head hinges on staying objective. Above all, don't be intimidated. It is crucial that the person does not perceive you as an easy strike or an accessible target. You must display a demeanor of readiness and strength to deal with whatever you're confronted with.

Most of your mental and physical energy should be concentrated on marshaling your skills and inner wherewithal to present a demeanor of calm and confidence. Another important point—don't get involved in situations where you have a personal attachment. You will think emotionally instead of rationally, and that could get you hurt.

Don't Make It Personal

My sister DeDe was real smart but sometimes attracted to the wrong crowd. I was always getting her out of something. I didn't mind—this was what brothers were supposed to do, and she always looked after me in every way she could. In the early years of my intervention work, she invited me to a party at her house one night to celebrate a job promotion. Everything went fine until just a few people were left, including the two guys who lived in the house with my sister and two other girls.

A dispute started just as I was about to leave. One of the guys hit DeDe and knocked her to the ground. I did a 180 and was met with a shotgun pointed at my chest. The brother cocked the gun.

"Don't," he said.

"Let it go, Aquil," DeDe begged from the floor. "Just let it go."

It was not the advice I wanted to hear but probably the best I could have received. I backed slowly out the door, not letting my cold stare leave the guy holding the shotgun.

The next day, DeDe came over with a big wire around her face. The dude had broken her jaw. I was enraged. Not only had this coward seriously hurt my sister, but he did it in front of my face and blatantly called me out. No way was I leaving it like that.

I went over to the house that night, packing a Mini-14 rifle and 9mm handgun. My sister's roommate appeared at the window, visibly upset, waving her hands and shaking her head "no." She pointed inside. I understood. There were other people in the house, innocent people. Just then the fool who was at the party cracked open the door, holding his hands up in the air.

"Where's that brother of yours? Tell him to get out here!" I yelled.

A minute later, someone slid the shotgun out the door and slammed it—a sign they didn't want any part of what I was bringing. I retrieved the gun, hollering, "It ain't over that easy. I'll be back." A week later those guys were gone and the house was up for sale. I never saw them again, but even today, I still think of them as a possible threat.

Today I would never utilize the actions I took that evening. I violated many of my own rules because I was personally involved in the situation. I damn sure wasn't thinking rationally, instead acting out of revenge and bruised pride. I could easily have gotten myself terminated.

If you are personally involved, your judgment is clouded. Emotion fogs your mental clarity, leads you to do things you never would normally. It falsely tells you that you can handle the situation and makes you ignore possible consequences that could get you and others injured or killed. You must let it go and walk away. Manning up is often about standing down.

Drink and Drugs

Interventionists should be especially careful when dealing with anyone who is on drugs or who they suspect has taken drugs. Even if they appear to act and speak normally, they are not operating in a state of mental normality—they are in an "altered level of consciousness," or what's known on the street as "ALC."

Their thinking is distorted, their rationale is impaired, their emotions are heightened, and their logic is diminished. You have to be extremely alert as to what the individual is doing and cautious in your actions toward them. Use as many of your proactive protocols as possible. ALC is a key risk trigger that can get interventionists injured or worse.

LEW

Lew liked getting high. Alcohol was his drug of choice although he was an equal opportunity substance abuser. He was a big dude and street savvy, but when he got loaded, all his smarts, common sense, and gut awareness went out the door and he became a bumbling bear. After a big payday binge on liquor and downers called red devils one Friday, Lew decided to pick up one of his regular girls who worked the street and take her home. When it came to time to pay her, Lew found his wallet was gone. He told her he would give her the money later and passed out.

(cont'd.)

I got a call from a young woman we had been helping to get her life to-gether—one of many. She told me I needed to get over to Lew's place fast, trouble was coming. Lew's regular girl had gotten a new pimp, an ex-banger who was fresh to the pimping game but possessed a vicious killer instinct. He was determined to make an example of Lew by taking him out.

I had just finished teaching a class at my martial arts academy. I shot over to Lew's with a couple students who were also on my intervention team. Luckily, we met the pimp in the parking lot; a few minutes later he would have been in Lew's apartment. The pimp knew of our work. He didn't like our efforts to get women out of the game, but he did appreciate the fact that we kept drugs out of the area and prevented many women from being beaten down by johns.

Because of that, he agreed to back off if we got him his money; that's all he really wanted. The bottom line is that Lew almost lost his life because he lost his common sense due to drugs and alcohol—we discovered later that he left his wallet at the bar. Startled after finding he had almost been killed, Lew joined a 12-step program and finally got sober.

Don't Be Superman

I've been threatened numerous times. I heard "I'm going to get you" so many times in my younger days, it was like the chorus of the number-one song on the radio. My response was always "bring it on" because I thought I was so damn bad.

One time this guy Bert thought there was something going down between his girlfriend and me, which was not the case at all. "You got yours coming," he would threaten. "I'm going to deal with you."

"Yeah, you and what army?" I shot back.

The situation finally defused itself when the couple broke up. I considered the matter closed and forgot about the whole thing. Not long after, I was supposed to be at a community event one night, but an emergency cropped up and I had to meet with my soldiers. Several of my friends went without me. They were driving out of the parking lot after the event, when someone fired at their car. One guy took four bullets to the head and died. I later got word from the street that the fools who shot up the car thought I was in it; I was actually their target.

I wondered if it was Bert. Sometime later, I got word that he had moved out of the city for no apparent reason. In the hood, that usually means he was fleeing something or someone. I wondered again if he had been behind the shooting. To this day I still perceive Bert as a possible menace. The only time a threat stops being a threat is when it has been neutralized in some way. The point is, with every threat you must take some sort of action.

In this line of work, making enemies is unavoidable. I'm very well known on the streets of Los Angeles, as well as in other communities across the nation. People know a lot more about me than I know about them. People can bear grudges or seek scapegoats for their problems, or they may be mentally disturbed. You just don't know. I now take every threat seriously and keep my responses low key. I advise my team to do the same. Don't issue challenges that other people may feel they have to live up to.

Intervention is a risky job, one in which danger is ever present and unpredictable. It's simply the nature of working in a world in which violence is a currency traded back and forth. We train and prepare for it as much as we can, but sometimes the outcomes can be tragic.

Joe had been watching the Super Bowl with his girlfriend at a bar on the west side of Los Angeles. After the game, he left the bar and spotted a tagger at work with a can of spray paint on a wall. He walked over and told the kid to stop. The teenager turned, drew a gun, and fired multiple shots. Joe died at the age of forty on the street.

The sixteen-year-old who killed him was quickly arrested with the help of a surveillance tape from a local business. Joe was a popular interventionist who had torn up the streets in his youth as a hardened gang member and then turned his life around and sought to bring peace to the very same streets. The fact that he had survived years of violence in gangs and prison and then met a violent death as a peacekeeper stunned the community.

Joe was trained as an interventionist, but his senseless death shows you can never know what or who you are dealing with all the time. The most you can do is take steps to minimize the danger to yourself and never take anyone or any situation for granted. Never think that your status as an interventionist means you are exempt from violence.

8 EMPOWERING COMMUNITIES: RESTORING FRACTURED NEIGHBORHOODS

Residents of South Los Angeles were upset. The city had approved a proposal to build a retail-condo development in an area that didn't get much interest from developers. The plan would bring badly needed jobs, housing, stores, and tax revenue, but residents thought it would lower property values and bring unwanted foot traffic to their tidy neighborhood of modest bungalows. Local gangs feared it would take away their turf, disrupt their activities, and flood the area with more police, while unemployed men felt they were being left out of the construction hiring.

Despite two community meetings on the issue, residents weren't backing down. Then-City Councilman Mike Williams, who was known for community outreach, scheduled a third meeting to hear concerns and try again to win local support. As he had done at the previous town halls, he asked me to provide safety for the event.

Before the meeting, a rumor was going around that local gang leaders were planning to commandeer the event because they felt Mike was arrogant and had disrespected them at the prior town halls. When I saw a grip of real players—gang members and unemployed men—marching to the church where the meeting was being held that evening, I knew it was for real. Among them was Al, a friend of mine.

"Brother Aquil, what you doing here?"

"We're here for the brother," I said.

"What brother?"

I mentioned Mike's name.

"Goddamn it!" Al said.

The hood reps told me their plan. People sitting in the front row were going to spring up during the meeting and surround Mike with large signs while others would seal the church's exits. The signal was going to be when a certain resident, who Mike had refused to let talk at the two prior meetings because he felt she disrespected him, stood up to speak. Once Mike literally was a captive audience, the reps were going to show him who had the real power in the neighborhood and tell him what was what.

Not wanting to disrespect my team and me by disrupting the meeting and making us look bad, they asked if we could leave for a while so they could carry out their strategy. I told them respectfully that was not an option. "We believe in what Brother Mike is trying to do for the neighborhood. There has to be a compromise here, and you guys have to talk. We need to work through this thing," I said.

The atmosphere in the hall was tense. Police cars circled the church and officers were gathering outside to flood the venue, which was making people uncomfortable. I asked a senior lead officer to lighten up on the uniforms, and because he knew my work and me, he agreed to leave just two officers inside and the rest would remain in the parking lot. The meeting started out civilly but soon heated up. Calm voices got louder, rebellious, and uncontrolled. I pulled aside Mike, whom I have known since high school. "You got to dial down your tone, and you got to let that lady talk tonight."

He refused. It had gotten too personal between him and her. I insisted. "You got to let her speak or this place is going to be turned upside down."

He still said no, but added that he would think about it. We went back and forth until reluctantly he agreed. "I'm only doing it because you asked me, Aquil."

To everyone's surprise, he let the woman speak. The homies got riled up but did nothing. Had things gone as they planned, Mike would not have been able to control that event. Violence more than likely would have erupted given the hot tempers and the heavy police presence.

» Community First Responders

To truly make an impact, professional interventionists must fulfill a larger role in the community beyond gang-violence disruption. They need to develop skill sets to deal with all kinds of issues and players in their communities—at-risk youth and schools, family dysfunction and domestic violence, mediation with law enforcement and other governmental agencies. They must be "professional community-intervention first responders."

The overarching ambition here is to restore besieged communities so they become self-reliant and can determine their own destiny. This includes empowering individuals to be activists and leaders, as well as turning around the mindset of individuals who use violence as a means to an end, both gang members and others.

Anyone aiming to work in a community under siege must understand that residents bear psychological effects from the high level of violence and trauma that makes life unforgiving and unapologetic in these neighborhoods. Neglected communities have a 22 percent higher level of trauma exposure than in suburban communities, similar to towns in war zones, says Robert Hernandez, adjunct assistant professor in the University of Southern California's School of Social Work. Robert often invites me to his classes as a guest speaker. "They're constantly in that fight-or-flight syndrome. It's cultural trauma," he says.

In response, people often self-medicate with alcohol, marijuana, and other drugs, and they tend to distrust outsiders after decades of neglect by officials, racism that has limited opportunities, and efforts by do-gooders who may be acting more for themselves than the community. "They are very guarded as to who they let into their community. The trust factor is a pressing issue," Robert says. "That's why interventionists are so important."

Many aspects of restoring a besieged community require changes in government policy and funding formulas—to reduce incarceration rates and overhaul schools, for example—but one key area that interventionists can directly tackle is reducing violence. A community cannot grow if children cannot walk safely to school, if businesses have to pay "taxes" to local sets, if people can't stroll the streets at night or play football in the park, if city workers are afraid to do their jobs. Violence chokes neighborhoods. Establishing peace is the vital first step in turning around communities. Peace forms the essential platform that allows other changes to occur and build from what already exists.

It should be noted that gang violence and community violence are different, although they can be linked. Gang violence is usually targeted. It is seldom random and is usually more brutal because it is inflicted to send a message or warning, or to instill fear. Community violence is more general in nature. It often occurs spontaneously, in the heat of the moment.

» Community Intervention and Restoration

Community intervention follows a four-stage process:

Stage 1: Reduce violence. A team of peacekeepers is trained and put in place to immediately defuse street and gang aggression. Street patrols are set up to detect and extinguish trouble before a crisis develops. For instance, peacekeepers are alerted by residents who cannot use a park because two gangs are warring over control of it. Interventionists get the gangs to agree to mediation and locate a safe house to conduct talks in a neutral, secure environment. The gangs agree to a ceasefire, and interventionists continue to monitor the ceasefire, stepping in to resolve disputes as necessary.

Stage 2: Establish and maintain community peace through measures to extinguish violence risk triggers. Interventionists working with community stakeholders establish safe zones throughout the neighborhood so all community members, both young and old, can feel secure in a healthy, violence-free environment. Interventionists conduct "impact sessions" with targeted high-risk youth to teach life skills and critical thinking. The aim is to change their acceptance of violence as a viable option for life achievement and self-esteem. Job training and placement must also be part of the formula in order to sustain the change in thinking. Interventionists train community members in the characteristics of gang violence and street aggression and how to combat it.

Stage 3: Evaluating risk factors causing violence. Interventionists convene a multidisciplinary collaboration of experts, such as mental-health services, housing, law enforcement, and various city departments to identify the root causes of violence and ways to combat it. This can include more recreational and job opportunities for youth; setting up safe havens such as homes, businesses, organizations where people can get away from the immediate threat of violence; graffiti removal; better street lighting; and community-oriented policing by officers who are local residents or grew up in the area.

Stage 4: Implementing a blueprint for long-term peace through proven community empowerment best practices. Schools expand afterschool programs to keep youth off the streets during critical hours of violence. Parks and recreation agrees to keep parks open late on weekends and include programs to boost the self-esteem and personal confidence of young adults, while local organizations such as the Boys and Girls Club and Police Athletic League organize sports activities. Public works carries out continual graffiti-removal and community clean-up programs. Community leaders establish an ongoing dialogue with public-safety officials aimed at building more constructive interaction with residents. Cops monitor hot spots and become a more visible deterrent force. City council representatives give residents a larger voice in infrastructure and building projects.

The community starts to flourish.

》 Community Engagement

Seattle was in the middle of a nerve-rattling outbreak of random homicides and violent crimes in three neighborhoods. City officials had beefed up police patrols and were advising residents to stay home and exercise caution when they went out. But the community wanted more action, and residents voiced frustration and fear at numerous town hall meetings. They wanted to know what else was being done and what they could do.

I had already been working in Seattle, training gang outreach workers who had made inroads in the established culture of gang and violent youth. But this fresh wave of violence was due to newer criminal elements appearing in the city—some were transplants from Los Angeles, some had nothing to do with gangs at all. I was brought in by the Seattle Youth Violence Initiative, the Seattle Seahawks, and the mayor's office to see what could be done.

I started by sitting down with key individuals and community organizations I had previously been working with, as well as reps from the mayor's office and public-safety agencies, to develop a list of concerns and ideas. The result was a community-empowerment plan that gave residents a role in creating their own public-safety environment.

I trained about forty volunteers as low-level "public-safety assistants" to work alongside the gang-outreach workers, social-service professionals, law enforce-

ment, and fire personnel. They learned how to control crowds at community events, to be conduits of information between police and fire officials and the community, to set up town hall meetings, and how to spot signs of impending violence, among other things. A nonprofit community-based organization, the Community Incident Safety Response Team, was formed as the volunteers' umbrella group.

Violence has gradually abated in the neighborhoods. Although the direct role the public-safety assistants have played in that is small, perhaps more importantly they symbolize hope and strength, a can-do spirit in the face of intractable social problems and the reality that neighborhoods are able to take charge of their own destiny and become self-reliant. Meanwhile, both law enforcement and city hall realized community members can be mobilized as a supplemental resource when given the proper tools of training and direction.

Stakeholder Buy-In

Getting buy-in from stakeholders is the essential first step to restoring any community. Community interventionists must reach out to a diverse array of individuals and organizations including churches, business associations, nonprofits, elected officials, residents groups, and police community-relations officers. Building those relationships—knowing who the key players are and their specific concerns—is paramount to forming a collaboration that not only strengthens community cohesiveness but also serves as a launching pad for grassroots movements.

Community interventionists must serve as a bridge between civic and political entities and the community and also be able to bring all parties to the table in private meetings, as well as public forums like town hall meetings. They also need to know who the right people are to bring to the table—people with standing in the community, officials in the agencies who have authority to take action on the concerns at hand, private funders. An important component of success is keeping stakeholders motivated and moving the process forward, as well as unifying the concerns and goals of the participants.

Community-Empowerment Format

A number of common denominators have been identified in successful community-empowerment projects. Here are some points to keep in mind:

- A clear understanding must be established that the overall need has to be the win for all involved. In Seattle, everybody won by stopping violence.
- The cause has to be large enough so stakeholders will sacrifice some personal gain for the greater good. City Hall had to find the budget for the public-safety-assistant training and volunteers had to give up time.
- Key community decision makers with proven credibility have to be at the table.
- A realistic plan has to be put forward with a clear end goal. Everyone must believe it will work.
- Deadlines to put plans in place must be specified and kept.
- The benefits must be clearly spelled out for each involved party.

Community intervention requires professional interventionists to develop a broader set of skills and interact with different players than they may be used to. It is important to put aside old hostilities and prejudices in order to move the work forward. In the end, everyone is pushing for the same goal—changing the dysfunctional thinking of those who use violence and turning communities into safer, healthier places.

9 BABY MAMA, BABY DADDY: HANDLING DOMESTIC VIOLENCE

Don was a good friend of mine who had a rocky marriage. He talked a lot to me about it, and I'd hear him out. He worked nights so he often asked me to stop by his house and check on his wife, Wendy, and their baby daughter. Wendy would take those opportunities to tell me her side of the story.

"One day, I'm going to terminate that bastard," Wendy said as we sat in the kitchen one evening.

"You need to quit that kind of talking," I replied, surprised at the depth of her feeling. Nevertheless, I really didn't take her seriously, and I later mentioned this to Don.

"She's just talking," he said.

"Yeah, I know," I said.

Their arguing never stopped. About two years later, they were arguing as usual one night, and it turned into a physical tussle. She took a butcher knife and repeatedly stabbed him, killing him in the bathroom. Mental-health professionals said she snapped. I don't know about that; the signs had been there, they just weren't taken seriously.

Wendy was convicted of second-degree murder, and the child went into foster care. If I had bet a $1 million on whether she'd carry out her earlier threat, I would've lost that money. I underestimated her, and so did her husband. Even if I had seen her with that knife, I still would've never believed she could do what she did.

After that I never underestimated any domestic conflict again. Any time I go into a domestic engagement now, my level of awareness is heightened and I brace for the worst. Interventionists will inevitably come up against domestic conflicts since they play a big role in neighborhood violence, sometimes even escalating into gang beefs. In my estimation, 70 percent of hard-core street situations involve three things: money, drugs, and "baby-mama drama."

The last one is the trickiest to navigate. These interactions are volatile and explode exceptionally fast because they're driven by emotion—often deep emotion—that overtakes any type of rational thought. People think with their hearts and act out of passion and impulse. Numerous factors are also usually at play that make these conflicts complex: children, outside family members, partners from past relationships, as well as elements such as physical safety, financial dependency, fear, and more.

» Getting Control of the Situation

The customary role of intervention specialists in dealing with domestic situations is not to solve the concerns that have led to the crisis but to get the parties through the crisis at hand. They attempt to guide the parties to some degree of temporary ease while connecting them to resources to resolve the underlying issues.

The first and foremost factor is controlling the emotionalism. This is often done by simply getting some physical distance between the parties so they can cool down. Once they regain their mental balance and start thinking rationally, the interventionist can then find out what the core of the problem is. Is it only one issue or many? Is this a problem between just the people on scene or does it also involve others who are not there? Can the issues be dealt with on the spot or is additional expertise needed? Does this have to be resolved urgently or is there time? What would each party like to happen as the outcome, and what would they be willing to accept as options?

Decide who will be your contact for the situation and if you will work with one of the parties or more. If more than one, you may need to call in colleagues to help out. You will also need more manpower if there is more than one threat or concern since each will need to be isolated. You must then consider the best technique to resolve the crisis: mediation, arbitration, bringing the parties back together, removing one or more from the scene, or a combination of these.

It's important to advise the parties to develop a support system of family and friends that they can turn to in the future to develop self-sufficiency, as well as refer to them to outside resources such as mental-health and medical professionals, shelters and agencies for battered women, housing and job placement aid, and transportation. Interventionists should always keep an up-to-date resource list at hand.

A word of caution. Domestic situations can fly off the handle in seconds, even when the parties have calmed down and the situation appears under control. People can lurch back and forth between coherent actions and thinking to uncontrolled emotion numerous times. Ready yourself for irrationality. Expect to be repeatedly searching for levelheadedness.

As with other conflicts, interventionists can find themselves targets in domestic disputes. Here are several precautionary measures:

- When entering the house, let them lead the way. Don't let them follow you.

- Never be led into a back, enclosed area like a yard. Stay near the front of the house, preferably in an open area.

- If you are inside, situate yourself close to the front or back door.

- Avoid the two most dangerous rooms in which to talk to the parties involved: kitchens and bathrooms. The kitchen houses knives, hot liquids, and utensils that can be used as weapons. The bathroom stores razors, possibly acids, and is a common hiding place for firearms.

- Look for signs of other people who may be in other rooms. Ask the parties if there is anyone else on the premises.

- Ask to use the restroom to try and get an overview of the layout of the house.

Domestic conflicts can involve all types of situations between all members of a household. These situations often require more patience than others because of the high emotions involved that can swing people back and forth between love and hate.

Situations that involve physical abuse call for an exceedingly gentle approach. You are dealing with women who have low self-esteem and live in fear, children who are traumatized, and men (sometimes women) who feel they have the right to exploit and dominate. Women who are being abused often have nowhere to go and no one to turn to. They are frequently psychologically battered, as well as physically, economically, and emotionally dependent on the abuser. Many will not leave the batterer, at least right away. They may believe they're in love with him and that he will change with time.

These situations can be frustrating, but it is imperative that interventionists remain nonjudgmental and keep their opinions to themselves. I have had to handle all types of domestic incidents and have learned to be flexible and open. It can be hard. One of the most personally trying situations I've ever handled involved incest, although it was successful from an intervention standpoint.

MALIK and KARIMAH

Malik and Karimah had been married for over two decades. They met in a religious institute and continued to be devout worshipers. They were considered one of the most upstanding families in their religious center. Their son, Sabir, had participated in my manhood-development program for about two years, as well as co-ed mentoring workshops. He was always filled with energy and passion, but then I noticed he became very subdued. I assumed it was growing pains. After five weeks of noticing this change in him, I pulled him aside, telling him that when he needed to dialog, I would be there for him. He nodded and left.

One evening his mother called me. "My husband's been abusing our son in a terrible way. I told Malik to call you, and fast. Sabir also wants to talk to you but he told me he didn't know how. I'm hoping you can help—I know how much they both respect you."

She refused to give me details. Two hours later, Malik called and we met. I was shocked at his confession—he had been sexually abusing his son for over six months. His wife found out when she came home one afternoon and found Sabir in extreme pain. He told her what his father had been doing. After confronting Malik, which turned physical, she took Sabir and left. Malik told me he was totally out of control and did not know how to stop his behavior even though he wanted to.

I got the son into counseling and a therapy program, and helped Karimah find housing and financial aid through her religious institution, and a job-

> **training program. I found an additional treatment program for Malik. The couple divorced. After recovering from the emotional and physical toll, Karimah remarried years later, and Sabir, with help from an excellent support group, graduated from college and is now married. Malik is still in therapy but has come to terms with his condition, which will probably require monitoring for the rest of his life. Thanks to therapy, the family still has contact with each other.**

As I said, be ready for anything, stay neutral, and control your own opinions and emotions.

» Counseling Jealousy

Beefs over jealousy drive a lot of violent incidents and can escalate into gang violence when homeboys take up the cause of a hurt homie. These situations require not only ending the back-and-forth hostility but some common-sense counseling to try to end the jealous behavior. The person has to be made to see that jealousy is a dead end and the object of their affections isn't worth fighting over, and definitely not going to prison for. The following scenarios provide an account of how intervention was utilized to handle common conflicts over jealousy, which is usually not directed at the object of affection but at the new person who has replaced the former partner.

The Neutralizing Process

Two sets of twin boys, who were members of rival gangs, were getting into fights practically every day after school. School officials figured it was a gang-rivalry beef and called in Penny Griffith, executive director of the Columbia Heights/ Shaw Family Collaborative in Washington D.C., a PCITI-trained community organization that works with youth and family. "We had busted eyes, busted noses, blood everywhere. They would stare at each other to start a fight," Penny says.

Penny sat down with the boys and soon found the constant fighting wasn't a gang beef at all. It was over a girl who had broken off with a brother in one set of twins and was now with a brother in the other set. Through a series of questions and several sessions, Penny got the jilted teen to admit there were other girls in the world and that it was possible he could like someone else. "I told them they had to be man enough to move on. They finally agreed not to stare at each other and to cross the street when they saw each other—and to find another girl."

Barbara Jett, a PCITI leader who became involved in a gang at the age of twelve and is now a major force in a female intervention peacekeeping team called Women Improving Neighborhoods (WIN), says jealousy over men is a major cause of infighting between girl gang members.

> **These guys move from one girl to another. It's all about the sex for them. But if they stay more than five minutes with one girl, then the last girl gets upset: "why didn't he do like that with me?" She doesn't see the problem is with him and not with the new girl. And the guy's there smiling; "They're fighting over me. I'm the man." And you know how it is with a fisticuff, everybody gathers round to watch. The men are just waiting for those blouses to come off.**

Fights can spark over nothing. Barbara handled one incident where a guy said hi to a girl in a store, which was witnessed by the guy's girlfriend's friend. She immediately reported back to her homegirl. The homegirls got together, jumped the other girl, and beat her down. "I get both sides together and the guy. When they see he doesn't care about one or other, they think about that. They see the reasoning." Barbara says.

» Changing Attitudes

Besides mediating domestic-violence crises, interventionists also tackle the issue at its roots—low self-esteem in girls, which can lead them into abusive relationships and keep them there, and ingrained disrespect in men toward women, which can lead to abuse.

A lot of our female interventionists specialize in working with girls and young women. Much of Barbara's work is teaching girls to value themselves for who they are—to base their sense of self-worth on what's on the inside, not on their ability to attract men by wearing skimpy clothing and being sexual objects. If they call each other "hos" and "bitches," men will treat them like that, she says.

"I teach them to respect themselves. I tell them to use different language, to put some clothes on. If you carry yourself differently, you will be treated differently. They come dressed differently the next time," Barbara says.

Far too often domestic violence is learned behavior. People who use violence in a dispute with their partners frequently grew up with it in their childhood homes. Men hit women because they saw their fathers do it, while women have learned to model the victim role of their mothers. It is seen as a normal relationship dynamic. Because this is learned so early in life, it is extremely hard to break the habit of resolving a disagreement with physical force, even if the parties are introduced to new options.

The gang mentality only reinforces the pattern of using physical force to resolve conflicts, responding fast to save face and acting Teflon-tough like nothing gets to you. Many gang members grew up without a strong father figure at home. Instead, they looked up to older homeboys and learned from them. While that may work in the gang, it doesn't work so well in outside relationships.

Gibran, a PCITI instructor, joined a gang when he was about fourteen. At fifteen, he robbed a bank and was locked up until he was twenty-six years old. A couple years after he got out, he married an English teacher. He quickly found he was lacking in the skills needed to make the relationship work. "I had to seek counseling and start working on myself," he says.

Gibran had to learn how to express himself and his feelings, how to handle conflict without walking out, how to think things over. "I didn't come from a traditional lifestyle. The way I was taught, everything had to be a yes or no decision. In the life, you act on impulse. I learned I don't have to make a hasty decision. I can say, 'let me think about it for ten minutes'."

Now he leads meetings for men convicted of domestic violence. Many of them grew up in violent households and learned early on not to respect women. Their aggressiveness is usually made worse by drugs and alcohol. Gibran also takes the counseling a step further, breaking the cycle by showing men how to be fathers because many grew up without dads. "They don't know how to interact with their kids. They were never taken to the park, so they don't think of taking their kids to the park. I show them they can do those things. You got to reteach them," he says.

I do a lot of counseling of men, trying to show them how to be better fathers, how to communicate better with the women in their lives. I point out that women carry a lot of responsibility—raising children as single mothers, being the lone family breadwinner when men have taken off or are locked up in prison, dealing with low-paying jobs and sexual harassment. The ongoing stress can make women blow up if an additional stress factor crops up. Men, just seeing the blowup, don't often realize that women have been pushed to that breaking

point. The typical male response of walking out while the woman is trying to be heard resolves nothing and in fact builds resentment, leading to worse blowups in the future.

My First-Hand Experience

I learned this the hard way. My wife and I have been married for thirty-nine years. Latifah's my best friend, my most supportive comrade, my lover, and the best backup a street soldier could ask for. We've had a very successful marriage, but not without challenges. We married young, in our early twenties, and it was real rocky for the first few years. One day we'd been arguing all day. We'd run out of words, so then it was just a stupid, silent mess, bumping as we passed by each other, things being dropped on the floor or kicked out of the way, glaring and making a show of avoiding one another. Somehow we both ended up in the kitchen. She was at the sink, and I asked her for a plate. She tossed it on the table, but it slid off and broke on the floor. "That was real smart," I said.

That was the opening she'd been waiting for. For the next hour, Latifah hit me with a barrage of pent-up complaints, following me around the house scolding me about everything I had done "wrong" over the past year. Finally I had had it. "Enough! I'm fed up with this bullshit! I need some air," I said.

She stood in front of me. "You're not going any damn where until I'm finished talking. You're going to hear me out once and for all. That's what's wrong with your ass, you're always walking away. You're a selfish punk!"

Her calling me a "punk" set me off. (To be fair, I had called Latifah certain names that were just as inappropriate—it was not one-sided, by any means.) I grabbed her by both arms, lifted her up, and sat her down hard on the kitchen table. I held her there for about five minutes, squeezing her arms and explaining to her why I was nobody's damn punk, what I did for her and our family, and why I wouldn't be disrespected like that. If this had been some fool in the streets calling me that, there would've been hell to pay.

Latifah kept saying, "Get your damn hands off me! Let me go! I'm not some damn fool in the streets, I'm your wife!" but I was determined to have her hear me out. I finally released her.

"You better not ever put your hands on me like that again or you'll seriously regret it!" she hollered.

"What the hell you gonna do, shoot me or something? Bullcrap!" I stormed out the house, jumped in the car, and was about to pull out when the backdoor swung open. "Hey fool, take this!" she said.

There was a loud bang. I was revving up the car, so I wasn't sure what it was. I drove to a nearby park to think. As I got out of the car, I noticed a hole in the door. I looked closer. It was a bullet hole, about five inches behind where I'd been sitting. My wife had popped off a round from the Smith & Wesson .38 that I had bought for her. I was astonished. I figured I was either extremely lucky or she purposely missed me. I wanted to think the latter. Latifah had been trained and certified in firearm use, and was too good of a shot to miss. She wanted to send a message, and she certainly did.

After that I did a lot of thinking. Had I been that callous, upsetting her to the point that she felt she needed to make a statement the way she did? Had I just brushed off her feelings and their importance? Obviously that had been the case. In the future I had to make sure to hear what my wife was saying. I had to truly listen.

I came to understand that we see things differently. My wife would want to spend time and talk a situation out, while I would want a quick answer and be done with it. I learned we could disagree and both be right. We didn't always have to have an answer right away, and some things take time. Patience was key, and this would have to be developed. Compromise was an integral part of the equation—you get your way sometimes, and other times you don't. I learned that regardless of who is right, it is the way you present the issue that matters most. Respecting each other as equals and not taking each other for granted is paramount to success. Integrity, trust, and keeping your word have to be part of the foundation. I have the best marriage I could have ever hoped for. It is not challenge-free, but we have agreed not to major in minors. If feelings become too heated, we walk away and revisit the issue later.

Domestic conflicts and violence are never easy to handle. They require a special skill set that combines both mediation and counseling techniques. Having interventionists on your team who have this specialty is crucial because relationship issues come up all the time.

10 COLORS ON CAMPUS: UNDERSTANDING THE SCHOOL DYNAMIC

I was busy at work one day when I got several calls from parents at my son's school where he was in the tenth grade. Word was going around that Amir was going to be jumped that afternoon by members of the local set. I was eighty miles away—there was no way I could've made it to the school in time—so I asked a close comrade, Big M, an O.G. from the sixties, to go there and make sure Amir got home okay.

He gathered three buddies, and they went to the school when class let out. Sure enough, they found a dozen gang members surrounding Amir in front of the school, ready to do some damage. Big M cleared that street and averted the confrontation, but we both knew it wasn't over.

When I got to the pad, I got the real deal. A number of sets were trying to establish themselves at the school and were recruiting members, mostly by force. Amir was being pressured to join one of them, but he was holding his ground. He had been taught to stand on his own, and that's what he was doing.

Although he had always come to me with any issues he had, he didn't with this one because he figured I would take action that would get me locked up. He did, however, inform school administrators. They told him he could wait with the counselors when school let out and leave an hour later, a response that was totally unacceptable. This would have made him more of a target and did nothing to prevent this from happening again.

These young gangsters didn't stop trying to jack my son. Soon after the first incident, I rolled up to the school to pick up Amir one day. As I waited in my truck, I saw him come out, and immediately about a dozen boys moved on him. I jumped out of the truck and planted myself directly in the middle of those chumps.

"Let me be clear to you young fools. The first one of you to move, I'm going to take you out."

"Who the fuck are you?" one asked.

"None of your damn business. I don't answer to no diaper-wearing, piss-ass fools."

Before he could respond, a voice from the crowd hollered: "That's Amir's father."

"You better check your damn son, he about to get his ass whooped," the ringleader said.

"Naw, I don't think so. You gonna need more than this so-called army you brought with you. First thing you better do is realize you're not dealing with one of your crew here."

The group slowly started to move away, mumbling snide remarks. "There gonna be another day!" one shouted.

Several parents who had witnessed the confrontation started clapping. "That was long overdue," one mother said. "These youngsters are totally off the hook. They've been causing trouble at the school for weeks; everybody seems to be afraid of them."

They told me this gang roamed in packs of five to ten, conducting random beatdowns, intimidating kids, taking their cell phones, money, and other items. Complaints had been made to school administrators to no avail.

I took this to the principal the next day. I had been to the school many times— they knew me by my first name. He actually admitted they needed help and asked me for assistance. I was staggered. I had expected excuses and resistance. After a few moments of silence, I outlined what I thought needed to be done, and he set up a meeting with district administrators.

Some of them had read about my work in an article in the local newspaper six months earlier and asked for my recommendations on dealing with this gang and other hostile youth. I convened a series of workshops for teachers and administrators over the following months to lay out strategies on handling gangs, bullies, aggressive youth, and campus violence. The school was finally able to clamp down on the gang activities, and I now had a respected working relationship with the district.

Gangs have always been a part of schools. Schools provide an ideal cover for many gang activities, including recruiting members, selling drugs, and warring with rivals, as well as shakedowns and robberies. If left unchecked, gangs can easily take over campuses and turn a place of learning and progress into a nucleus of dread and fear. Over the years I have collaborated with numerous schools throughout Los Angeles County and elsewhere in Southern California to develop antiviolence and proactive safety programs.

》Gang Infiltration

If a school is located in a community with gangs, you can be assured that school will also have gangs. Teachers and administrators usually have little training or experience in dealing with the gang culture. The lack of preparation, and sometimes even denial that a gang problem exists, makes schools a fertile breeding ground for gang philosophy. The level of gang infiltration depends on how attuned administrators are to the problem and how seriously they take the threat, if the school has a critical response team and a safety plan, and the school's level of collaboration with the community.

Teachers and administrators can find valuable allies in parents when dealing with troubled youth, but parents are not always available in inner-city neighborhoods. Often there is only one parent in the house, sometimes none. Some parents may be too overwhelmed with the daily demands of hand-to-mouth living to be able to deal with an additional challenge or are simply at a loss as to how to rein in their kids.

There are other issues, too. If the community has longtime, well-entrenched gangs, school personnel will come up against families with two or more generations who have been involved in the life. Many of these parents, although not all, take pride in being part of the culture and will often be useless in turning around the mindset of the young adult involved in gangs. They may have even encouraged their children to join the family set.

There are measures a school can take to diminish gang influence. The first thing adults must learn is how to spot gang infiltration at a school. Note that just because students wear baggy clothing and have tattoos does not mean they are gang members. Other indicators must be present as well. Here are some of the more common signs, although each school setting will have its own indicators that need to be identified:

Indicators of Gang Presence

\# Areas of the school grounds have become segregation zones, where only certain students appear allowed to go and others tend to stay away from. Sometimes these are out-of-the-way spots such as niches or behind or between buildings, but they can also be places out in the open.

\# Open congregations of students at the front or rear doorways and the reluctance of other students to use those doors.

\# Physical and mental intimidation by groups of students, or targeted pupils being continually pressured and jumped, causing them to become withdrawn.

\# Shutdown by students when asked by adults what is going on, failure to inform adults of harassment or threats (indicating fear of reprisal), and the reluctance of students wanting to go to school.

\# Constant reference to a particular student or students by peers, which indicates a hierarchy or caste system is in place.

\# Specific students regularly picked up from school by groups of older adults who seem to fit the gang lifestyle.

\# Unwarranted aggression and defiance toward school adults. Displays of arrogance—a "you don't know who you're messing with"–type attitude—showing an expectation that street status be respected at school.

\# Certain students using a lot of slang talk. Wearing the same, unusual items such as nylon belts with the same key chains hanging from them, white or colored oversize T-shirts, or items with innocuous-seeming insignia like baseball teams every day. The items can change from day to day.

All schools will have some or all of these characteristics to some extent, so it will take alert observation by teachers to detect if there is any "representation," or affiliation with the local sets, present. Regardless, schools need to do what they can to eliminate these negative tendencies so they don't occur in the first place.

Measures can include: establishing a confidential anonymous tip line, website, or other means to report extortions, provocation, or illegal activity; having a resource network to quickly connect students to social services and other help; establishing a dress policy that bars local gang colors or insignia. Teachers should make note of who the student ringleaders appear to be, who gets picked up from school by young adults, who could be gang couriers. That information may be needed if there is trouble on campus and administrators need to talk to ringleaders.

An imperative is controlling campus access and grounds. All entrances and exits should be monitored, and whoever comes on or leaves the compound should be noted by security personnel. This includes outlying areas such as athletic fields and parking lots, as well as buildings, interior walkways, and courtyards. If possible, limit access to one main gate.

School compounds can be color-coded to clearly specify the areas where students, parents, and other visitors are allowed to go, and signage indicating this should be prominent. Hidey-holes on school grounds where assaults and drug use and dealing can occur must be identified and monitored. The school grounds should be walked by a two-person adult team throughout the day and student bathrooms spot-checked regularly. In cases where budgets do not stretch to hire security personnel, parent volunteers can sometimes be tapped to serve as monitors.

Although schools do not want to look like fortresses and should be open and inviting, in high-crime, gang-infested neighborhoods, steel-bar perimeter fencing is a good investment to ensure safety.

» Safe Passage, Safe Houses

Pokey, a young gang member, had been executed in what looked like a targeted assassination by a set of rivals from a nearby hood. He had recently graduated from a middle school that drew students from four adversarial neighborhoods. When Pokey's death sparked the inevitable, all-out retaliation by his homeboys, the school immediately felt the impact, on and off campus. Fights, vandalism, truancy, shootings, beatdowns, and general classroom disorder soared.

Teachers and administrators were exhausted, as were local residents and parents, who were pressing the school to take action. Administrators had heard of my team's work at other schools and called us for help. That resulted in a partnership with the Los Angeles Unified School District to evaluate twenty-six gang-neighborhood schools and train personnel in gang intervention, hostility and aggression, violence-abatement procedures, and school safety.

Safe Passage

We went further than that and created the district's first comprehensive "safe passage" program, which later became "Safe Journey," aimed at preventing gang infiltration of schools. The program has been replicated numerous times in other school districts and, I'm proud to note, is still in use today.

We came up with the safe passage program after evaluating the schools and finding one of the biggest problems was that kids were afraid to walk to and from school. Even as young as elementary schoolers, they would get robbed, pressured to join local sets, or have drugs and alcohol offered to them en route. If they refused, they would get threatened or assaulted. Since the incidents didn't occur on school grounds, the school had no jurisdiction. This became the cornerstone issue in creating a program to deal with gangs.

Our first step was bringing together community stakeholders, school officials, professional gang interventionists, and city administrators. We drew up a crisis map to pinpoint the "hot spots," where violent incidents were occurring around the school, and then mapped out routes from the school's feeder neighborhoods within a two-mile radius that avoided those hot spots. Through community leaders, residents were asked to act as "scouts on post" before, during, and after school. At intervals along the routes, the residents were asked to stand sentry in their driveways or front yards as a deterrent and to report any trouble to authorities.

Safe Houses

The next step was establishing a system of safe houses. Residents and selected business owners were asked if their premises could be used as safe houses for youngsters or anyone else in distress or fleeing violence. The idea was that people would have a confidential refuge until the source of harm has abated or gone.

The safe house can connect people to outside resources, and provide food and a bed for the night if necessary. Schools, community centers, and fire stations have also served as safe houses. The tricky part is keeping the location of the safe houses as secure as possible. Usually they are known in the community by word-of-mouth. Sometimes a business might put a yellow placard in the window indicating that it is safe haven.

Additional Components

To deal directly with local gangsters, professional peacekeepers were hired to start a dialogue with set leaders to declare schools off limits for gang activities and leave children alone on their way to school. Interventionists also patrolled the safe passage routes to ensure gangs were not breaching them.

Another component was launching afterschool programs to teach at-risk youth life skills and turn around the dysfunctional thinking process of gang culture. My program, B.U.I.L.D. (Brotherhood Unified for Independent Leadership through Discipline) for both boys and girls, includes "impact sessions," motivational talks by former gang members and others, as well as frank, confidential discussions of issues young adults face at home and school as a way of venting and finding support.

Another of our programs—F.I.R.M. (Fathers Involved in Redefining Men)— is a manhood-development curriculum specifically aimed at boys without fathers. Participants learn about leadership, responsibility to the community, the importance of being an effective father, keeping a family together, and other life skills.

We also developed community response teams and crisis crews composed of parents, volunteers, prevention experts, school administrators, and public-safety responders. The response team is trained to respond to low-level general situations, such as a student protest on campus and events needing crowd control, while the crisis team is trained to handle more serious situations such as a classroom hostage situation or a riot.

Local gang-intervention specialists should be incorporated into the teams. It should be noted that although some interventionists have felony records and are barred from working in schools, they can help from the outside by quelling gang tension that spills over to the school. Interventionists who do not have felony records can play larger roles by participating in school-based activities.

» School Shootings

Sadly, school shootings, by students and adults, have become all-too-common in our society today. Short of putting airport-style metal detectors at the entrance of every school, which some high-violence schools have done for many years, there is no surefire way of preventing people from bringing guns on campus. There are, however, ways to protect students and teachers from an active shooter. These should be detailed in a school safety plan that assigns tasks and courses of action to specific school personnel in the event of a crisis.

Controlling who comes onto the campus, as detailed in the previous section, is a key security buffer, and many schools now require visitors to sign in at the main entrance. But care should be taken to secure access around the perimeter of the school grounds and monitor it. There are usually many ways to get onto a school campus, and people determined to do so will find them.

Many recent cases involve shooters who are students themselves, which makes access an irrelevant point. I recommend that schools go a step further—equip each classroom with some type of emergency alert system, such as a silent, color-coded light system with each color signifying a specific crisis. Teachers should be able to discreetly but easily activate the system, which would be connected to the front office or school police officer, if there is one. I also urge that teachers keep doors closed, if not locked, when class is in session.

It is also vital to have a safety plan and hold scenario-driven drills at least once a semester so students and teachers are well versed in what to do in specific situations, such as if someone with a gun is on campus. The safety plan and drill should include the following elements:

- If a classmate takes out a gun, immediately drop to the floor, facedown. A gunman shoots from midsection height, rarely aiming at the floor.
- Overturn desks, cabinets, or other furniture, and position yourself behind them as cover. Try to locate any solid object that would stop a bullet.
- Move to a far wall immediately if gunfire is heard in the hallway or another classroom. Refrain from looking out the window in the door or staying near the door and facing the classroom.
- Equip each classroom with basic emergencies supplies, including food and water, to last at least a 24-hour period.
- If a shooting takes place outside, on a playing field for example, run fast from the shooter in a zigzag fashion, or bobbing your body up and down. Shooters are rarely trained to strike moving targets.
- Designate a "safe zone" where students, teachers, and parents can report to in a crisis.
- Stress repeatedly to students that they must inform an adult of any rumor, conversation, or implied threat of a shooting, bringing weapons to school, or suicide, even if they think the person is just joking.

» One-on-One Intervention

In my opinion, gangs and violence have worsened in schools over the years. There is no question that gangs themselves have become more brazen and vicious as they have become increasingly sophisticated with their weapons and communication via social media. But I also place a portion of the blame on schools themselves and the zero-tolerance disciplinary policies used by many districts across the nation.

When gang-affiliated youth are suspended or expelled, often for trivial matters, the first place they go is the streets. With an additional chip on their shoulder over the disciplinary action, they become even more hardened. When they return to school at a later date, they bring this reinforced hardened mentality with them, creating a bigger problem in the school environment.

Interventionists can play a unique role in disrupting this cycle. They can talk to youngsters not only from experience but also straight from the heart. Many interventionists were once those kids themselves. That's a valuable asset when dealing with at-risk youth, who can be hard to reach often because childhood emotional trauma has caused them to wall themselves in against the outside as a defense.

Luis Cardona, a close friend and partner in PCITI's Regional Gang Intervention Certification Training program in Maryland, holds "healing circles," where kids sit in a circle and talk about the trauma in their lives without fear of being judged.

Luis brings his own experience to the table. Anger over being sexually abused as a child led Luis to join a gang when he was eleven. Gangs, he says, thrive on angry kids. "It's the gladiator syndrome. What better way to unleash that bottled-up anger and pain than on rivals?"

After going through a revolving door of homes for emotionally disturbed children, juvenile correctional institutions, and prison, burying thirty-five of his friends, being shot five times, and leading a gang as shot caller, Luis left the life two decades ago. He earned a college degree in political science and is now youth violence prevention coordinator for Maryland's Montgomery County Department of Health and Human Services. "The healing piece is so important, the ability to deal with your own pain and baggage. Once they heal, it doesn't mean the pain is gone, but they respond differently," he says. In other words, without violence.

Other interventionists use different ways to reach at-risk youth. Blinky Rodriguez, whom I mentioned previously and who lost a son to gang violence and now runs nonprofit Communities in Schools outside Los Angeles, gets rival gangs to blow off steam by playing each other in Sunday football, basketball, and other sports events. It's a way of getting rivals to relate to each other as human beings rather than as nameless targets for bullets.

The games preserve the competitive spirit between gangs so they don't feel pressured to be friends with the enemy. Nonetheless, seeing each other close up helps break down the depersonalization process that makes gang members able to kill rivals because they have learned to see them as objects, not as people with families and aspirations like themselves.

Being Role Models

One of the most important ways interventionists can help kids is by simply being role models. "Just like there are role models in the negative life, there are models in the positive life," says PCITI interventionist and instructor T Top Rivers, who joined a gang when he was about eleven and turned his life around after coming out of prison when he was twenty-seven.

I stress in my classes that leading by example is the best way to show youths a way out of gang life. These are kids who may never have had a positive role model—the adults in their family may be gang members, incarcerated, have substance abuse problems, or may never have held a real job.

T Top knows firsthand that it's not easy to sway young people from a lifestyle that seems to offer everything: money, respect, girls, cars, a sense of family:

> A lot of youngsters don't like peace. They got to keep up that hard image, that tough persona you have to have in that lifestyle. They say, "Who wants to live in poverty?" I say, "Who wants to live watching over your shoulder, walking up to your house wondering if you're going to be shot by someone you went to junior high school with? And with the police on your back, it's a no-win situation." I've taken a lot of hits—they say I'm getting soft, getting old. But I'll take those hits. I say, "I'm not asking you to go hang out with the Bloods, just give us and our community a chance to live, to build a community and let kids grow and not be incarcerated.

I couldn't have said it better myself.

11 LOCKUP: ADJUSTING TO LIFE IN AND OUT OF PRISON

2Shot was a straight up killer. Vicious, merciless, completely unapologetic. He got his name by way of the two bullets he would always put in his victims. "If I can't kill 'em with two, they deserve to live," he used to say.

2Shot had grown up hard in a series of foster homes. He would run away and live off the streets till he got caught and sent back, then he'd run away again. Around the age of sixteen, he ran away and never went back. To survive, he joined the local set and quickly became one of its top shooters, gaining notoriety for the ferocious nature of his killing. He would take people out on "GP"—general principle, just for the sake of it. He liked killing, plain and simple.

I despised 2Shot with a passion. A close comrade of mine had been severely wounded in a shooting that had left two others dead. My buddy fingered 2Shot and two others as the shooters, but he was never charged due to a lack of evidence.

One day I heard 2Shot had been arrested in the brutal murder of an entire family behind a drug deal gone bad. One of his homies had supposedly dropped a dime on him (told authorities) for a lighter sentence. 2Shot went down for manslaughter. He went berserk in the courtroom, swearing he was going to kill anybody who had anything to do with his conviction, as well as their families. "All of you will better watch your motherfucking backs!" he hollered.

Years passed and I was working in the federal prison system holding workshops for inmates on life skills, re-entering society, and the like. I was at the prison one Saturday for a special presentation for African-American History

Month, when I heard my name being called. I turned around and saw a vaguely familiar figure approaching. As he drew closer I recognized him—2Shot.

I stared at him for a minute—I could see he was still hard as hell, but his eyes had lost their fire after years of being locked up. He stuck out his hand and we shook, although I remained on the defensive. We walked to the back of the room. He said he held no grudges with me but still wanted vengeance on the people who put him behind the wall. He claimed he was set up. I found that hard to believe, but he stuck with it.

"I heard you were working in the prisons," he said. "I've been trying to get in contact with you. I'm getting out in less than a year, looking for some assistance."

I could see he was no longer the same man who ran amok in the streets, and I decided to leave the past where it lay for the moment and fulfill my purpose of helping rehabilitate inmates. "We can talk about what you need," I said.

Over the next six months, I saw 2Shot about five more times, counseling him about his upcoming release and even developing a friendship. I felt he was making real progress except for the issue of his wanting revenge. He was hell-bent on getting even. The breakthrough came right before his parole. We heard the guy who had dimed him out had AIDS and had a maximum of two months to live. The news had an unexpected effect on 2Shot. He opened up to me one evening in the conference room:

> Damn, I kept saying to myself over and over, year after year, I am gonna get that damn clown. Now I'm about to get out, this clown is about to die. I've wasted over a decade on hate and retaliation. I could have used that energy to build myself into something better. No more, never again, I'm done!

2Shot seems to have stayed true to his word. When he was released, I connected him with a GED program and some individuals in the halfway house to mentor him and possibly get him a job if he stayed clean. I have never again heard his name in connection with anything negative. He now has a family with two small sons.

Change is possible. The impetus to change has to come from within the person, but he or she has to have support from the outside to guide them and hold them accountable. That's why I started my Behind the Wall incarceration intervention program, which takes what I call a "trilateral" approach: before, during, and after prison.

Prisoners, ex-prisoners, and their families are largely a forgotten group in our society. The public tends to have a "lock 'em up and throw away the key" attitude, which is counterproductive. If offenders and their families don't get support, they will simply commit more criminal acts, creating new victims and returning to prison at taxpayer expense. That's why I consider working with this group an essential part of my mission to control and end violence.

» Back in the Hood

Recidivism is one of society's problems that never seems to get solved to any reasonable degree. To me, the key to preventing people from returning to a life of crime and violence is meeting their basic needs: housing, employment, societal adjustment, and mental-health and drug-treatment services.

Of course, a certain percentage of people will choose violence no matter what, but there are more people who, if given the right resources when they are released from prison, will become productive citizens. It is not easy—ex-offenders are often starting from zero when they're paroled. They have considerable needs that adults who have taken more productive paths in society have generally taken care of long ago.

The Behind the Wall program provides mentoring and counseling for parolees by role-model interventionists who have come out of prison and successfully turned their lives around. We help them with practical issues like adapting to changes in society during the time they've been inside—cell phones, the Internet, debit cards, to name a few—and emotional ones, like making their own decisions after years of being told when to get up, when to eat, when to go to bed. Some people have difficulty adjusting to the sudden freedom of choice and may think life was easier in prison. Overwhelmed, they seek refuge in negative behaviors such as drug use, which can land them right back behind bars. We try to provide them the support and guidance to cope without turning to drugs and alcohol.

Family Reconnection

Reconnecting with family can be another emotional obstacle. Many former inmates say renewing family ties is one of the most difficult things about returning to the street.

Anthony, a PCITI peacekeeper who figures he has spent a total of over twenty years in juvenile and adult institutions, says the hardest thing about coming home from prison the last time was finding he had no home. Not only did his house and all his belongings burn down a couple years earlier, but also his family wasn't exactly putting out the welcome mat. "My wife and kids had moved on with their lives. I had left them one too many times," he says.

He went to a halfway house and became determined to build back his life without the gangs that he was involved in since the age of nine—he founded his own gang when he was twelve. "I took money-management classes, anger-management classes, something every day to keep me positive. I took advantage of everything they had to offer and started connecting to new people." Those connections gave him the encouragement and support he needed to reach his goal of starting a new chapter in his life. "When people see you're trying to do something better with your life, they will help you," he says.

Debra Warner, an associate professor of forensic psychology who has worked with ex-offenders and has collaborated with PCITI, says reconnecting with family sometimes isn't possible. "It's very important to have somebody. Sometimes it's not blood. I ask them who their kinfolk relatives are—the people they called 'auntie' or 'cousin.' It can be a pastor or clergy. I try to find anybody will be supportive of them."

Employment Dilemmas

The lack of jobs is maybe the biggest factor that pushes people back into the life. Many guys have never held a real job or have no marketable skills. All they've done are things like mop floors and serve meals in prison. On top of that they now possess a felony conviction, which bars them from most formal employment. We locate employers who are willing to take a chance on ex-offenders or those who enroll in state programs that give tax breaks for employing them. Still, the demand for jobs far outstrips the supply.

PCITI interventionist Reno, who spent thirty years in prison for a gang-related murder, learned electrician skills in prison. When he was released, he got a job as an electrician, but it took time and wasn't easy. "Employment was the hardest thing. I was on GR (general relief welfare) for a couple months. A lot of guys get frustrated and go back to the block. Then the police come and they got their job to do. There's a cycle going on. You gotta have a strong mindset, a strong will and determination to make it. It's a lot what you have up against you. You need resources, that's the bottom line."

It's important to find out the person's natural skill sets and apply them to what type of job they could do, says Dr. Warner, who has a PsyD and sits on the board of directors of the National Partnership to End Interpersonal Violence Across the Lifespan. A person who ran a drug dealing operation probably has entrepreneurial and leadership talent, for example. But she underlines that attitude is the key to whether a person will change:

> How they see themselves is very, very important. If you believe crime is all you can do, you're going to keep doing it. You have to change their thinking from "I'm not worth anything, I'm not smart enough to do anything" to "if I try hard enough, I can learn to read, I can get my kids back." I try to change their picture of the world, but they have to want to change.

Part of the process is finding out where they got the negative view of themselves in the first place. Dr. Warner says:

> I listen to their stories. There's a lot of untreated trauma—violence, sexual abuse, drug addiction—that causes people to go different routes in society because they don't know how to handle it. Some had parents in and out of the corrections system, so that was their normal. They don't believe they can do anything different.

Anthony says he advises guys to persevere, but he knows some will give in. "Temptation is always going to bite you in the ass. Some guys have no choice but to go back to life. That's all they know. You have to do what you have to do to survive. I tell them be persistent, never give up. It's up to you what you do with your life."

» The Pen

We start trying to change the mindset when individuals are still in prison or jail. I do a lot of work inside penitentiaries, in the Los Angeles County adult and juvenile corrections systems and the federal prisons in California. I have also worked in the California state penal system. The cornerstone of my work with inmates is holding what I call "impact sessions" with groups of about fifteen to twenty inmates. We sit in a circle formation in a classroom and address life and survival-skill topics depending on the needs of the group.

In the county jail I counsel inmates about to be released on subjects such as how to get your credit rating cleaned up, developing a better relationship with your wife, and how to be a better father.

New prison inmates need to know how to navigate culture in the pen to avoid beatdowns, setups, and back stabbers. These may be small things in the outside world, but in prison they take on undue importance:

* who to talk to
* who is affiliated with what
* what part of the dorm is off limits
* when to respond verbally to other inmates, when to shut up
* what area of the yard is restricted
* what key phrases mean, being careful what you say
* who you can confide in, who to avoid
* what type of guards to stay away from
* how to stay focused without losing your mind
* where and how to stand in the shower
* how to wear prison garb
* "killspots" to avoid throughout the prison

I also try to mentally prepare them for the isolation. In jail, inmates know each other and institutions are local, making it easy for families to visit. But prisons, especially federal institutions, can be located far from inmates' homes, and families may not be able to visit often.

Prisoners need to know how to handle emotional goodbyes to their loved ones at the end of visits. They need to be ready for the possibility that marriages and relationships will end, that they may become strangers to their kids. I also connect them to legal advice about appealing their convictions, which inmates must do on their own if they do not have money for a private attorney.

The sessions often naturally turn into therapy groups. I've found inmates seize the chance to unburden themselves. I try to instill hope and optimism by leaving them with little constructive sayings such as "through adversity comes greatness" to remind them we have to sacrifice for things worth having, and "the past doesn't equal the future" to keep them looking forward, not backward.

Juvenile Inmates

Juveniles get more of a mentoring session on turning their lives around before it's too late. I also try to alter their mindset of embracing violence to accepting socially positive alternatives. Sad to say, I've run into some young men each step of the way as they progress through the corrections system, from juvenile hall and probation camps to adult jail and then prison. But there are success stories that keep me motivated.

PJ

PJ had been trapped in the revolving door of the juvenile corrections system for years. He started young, stealing cars and stripping them down. He then moved up to breaking into small airports to steal hydraulics lifts off planes. He'd sell them to local people with lowriders, cars with lowered suspensions that made them sit low to the ground, so they could "lift" the cars and make them bounce up and down on the pavement to impress onlookers. PJ got busted numerous times, but because he was a juvenile, he would do a few months and be back on the street. I started working with PJ in Juvenile Hall. He was a tough nut to crack, and normally I might have moved on, but I saw potential in him. He was ingenious, but he had always been surrounded by individuals who never encouraged him to use his intelligence for positive undertakings. It took over a year before I got a sign that we were making progress.

"You're really not going to give up on me, are you?" he said one night as I sat in his dorm with him.

I shook my head. "No."

He looked at me. "I know you have a son my age, Brother Aquil. You spend all this time with me and you could be spending it with your son, does he ever get mad? I feel bad, you shouldn't be with me, you should be with him. I thought I'd never say this, but seeing how you put in this work with me, I owe it to you and your family to give something back. I'll make you proud one day and I keep my word."

It was a special moment, and I was moved. After PJ was released, he went back to school. He later opened a series of safe havens for homeless and recently incarcerated young adults, which he still operates today. By the way, PJ and my son became friends.

Juvenile Institution Safety

My corrections work includes training school teachers who work in juvenile facilities on classroom safety. This includes strategies such as:

- positioning the instructor's desk near the door to be able to exit fast but without blocking access for the class
- using the desk as a buffer between a student and the instructor
- breaking up fights without getting physically assaulted
- reading body language, such as bouncing up and down on toes or hitting a fist into a hand, to detect an impending emotional explosion
- learning the meanings and usage of street slang
- developing a classroom safety plan for emergencies

Additionally, I show teachers how to talk with their students and develop a rapport with them by identifying their needs and wants, and providing practical options if those needs can't be met right away. Sometimes these relationships have flourished outside the detention facility so the teacher becomes a needed mentor or guide who keeps the youth on the right track.

》Families

Families of prisoners are the unseen, unheard victims of the crime and punishment cycle. Incarceration can devastate families, especially when a breadwinner is sent away for a long stretch. The entire family structure undergoes upheaval. The most common side effect I see is that a family is plunged into poverty. Women frequently become the sole support of families. Sometimes they can't make it. They get evicted and have to move in with parents or other relatives.

Older children may have to assume responsibility in the home for younger siblings or earning money, sometimes dropping out of school to get a job or resorting to crime to make ends meet. Some children of incarcerated parents get angry at the system for taking away their parent and take out their emotions in acts of aggression and violence at school and home.

On top of that, the inmate becomes a new burden. They call home wanting money in their prison account, favorite foods, books and TV sets, and so on. Visits can require long drives, hours of standing in lines, searches, and being bossed around by guards. Prisoners may unload sadness and frustration on family members, so relatives come away feeling guilty and depressed, or angry at being made to feel that way.

I've worked with countless families, directing them to resources that can provide everything from free bus transportation to prisons to food and clothing. I also instruct them on how the prison system works, visiting procedures, what they can bring, and so on, as well as what the prisoner is going through inside. I counsel them, using the concept of "steel sharpens steel"—that incarceration puts the inmate under pressure to come out better than before, to be polished through a process of fire, if you will. I have found that perspective provides families with some degree of solace.

Working with inmates and parolees on turning their lives around can be slow and frustrating. But seeing someone become a productive citizen after a life of wreaking harm and destruction is truly rewarding. The upside is that all of society benefits. I only wish more politicians and policymakers would see it this way.

12 STREET-SAVIOR SYNDROME: SURVIVING THE EMOTIONAL TOLL

I was in a park on L.A.'s west side to do some mediation between two gang sets involved in ongoing war. It was a sunny Saturday afternoon, and the park was full of kids playing ball and chasing each other. Out of nowhere, a series of deafening cracks ripped through the air. A drive-by. Everybody screamed and bolted.

As I sprinted for cover, I spotted a little girl lying near the jungle gym in a pool of blood. I switched course and rushed over to her. She had been almost sliced in half by bullets from an AR-15, a semiautomatic assault rifle. I tried to hold her together until paramedics arrived, but she was like an exploded rag doll. Flesh and tissue were scattered around the playground. Blood flooded out of her, soaking her dress. There was no way she was going to make it, still I couldn't let go of her.

With sirens whooping in the distance, I thought of the sheer senselessness of losing such a young life before it even had a chance to be lived. I thought of my own two daughters and the agony I would be in if this were my little girl. I was overcome with guilt that there was nothing I could do to save her. She was about nine years old.

When I got home, I took a shower and stood under that water for what felt like hours, trying to cleanse myself of the evil of violence, I guess. When I finally got out, the only thing I could do was drop to my knees and pray. That little girl still haunts me today. It is another of the incidents that drives my power to keep going in this work to end violence.

I truly view violence and crisis intervention as my life's mission. It is the purpose of my existence. But there is no doubt that besides physical danger, it takes an emotional and physical toll and requires a lot of personal sacrifice. This is work that you must be driven by the heart to do. It takes a rare kind of personal commitment to expose yourself to constant stress, trauma, and heartrending setbacks, especially when there is little or no recognition when you succeed.

》Dealing with Letdown

Many people think they can do this work, but they quickly find it is much more demanding than they realized. The emotional pitfalls are the hardest part to overcome. It can be downright depressing when you put your soul into the work and you keep running up against a brick wall. I saw people going out to kill someone based on an unverified rumor or because "that's how my father done it, my grandfather done it." People at the table accept the terms of a peace deal but then turn around. "We can't do this."

"Why not?"

"It's not just the way we do it."

Many a time I thought I had resolved a situation only to hear the next day that innocent babies and elders got wasted. I've had occasions when people gave me their word and an hour later there was a gang war. I've seen a young person who was on the right path get a life sentence for making senseless, uncaring choices. There were times when my presence made the situation worse—I wasn't impartial enough when friends were involved. I'd get disgusted by hypocritical peacekeepers doing the work for personal glorification, money, and fame. I wondered what the point of me being out there was. Numerous times I said, "Fuck this!" and walked away.

What always called me back was the guilt that somebody could die if I didn't keep going. I'd remember that little girl in the park or my brother, and I'd tell myself his death and those of many others could not be in vain. If I could save just one more life, save one more mother or father from going through the agony of losing a child, my efforts will have been worthwhile. I'd reach deep within myself and from some unknown place find the wherewithal to pick myself up and go back out there. And the successes make up for all the disappointments. Reno, a PCITI interventionist, sums it up in simple words: "When you save one person, it's the greatest feeling in the world."

The best interventionists are those who can deal with what my close friend Blinky Rodriguez describes as the "manic-depressive rollercoaster" because they view the work as a vocation. They are going to do it no matter what.

PCITI interventionist T Top Rivers says he feels his gangbanging past was almost like preparation for his current role. "I have a calling for it. God sent me through what I went through to have a voice," he says. Others say the work is atonement for the harm they did as a gang member and offers a path to redemption. "I helped destroy my community. I was part of that problem. I have the responsibility to make it better," says Anthony, another PCITI interventionist.

Luis Cardona, a PCITI-trained interventionist and instructor in Montgomery County, Maryland, says he's convinced that he survived five bullet wounds and near death while a gang member for a purpose: "There is no doubt in my mind that God put me on this earth to do what I'm doing."

Motivated by deep personal dedication, interventionists can easily fall into a mindset of feeling overresponsible for others and believe they are indispensable. They can take on too much, constantly push themselves, rarely admit when they are overwhelmed, absorb more than they can handle. But in order to survive in this discipline, it is essential to take measures to take care of yourself to avoid the real pitfall of burnout. This work will consume you if you let it.

》Setting Limits

Setting boundaries is crucial to keeping your balance. You must draw lines and stick to them. This includes establishing limits on your time and energy. You have to realize when you've done all you can do and it's time to go home and make sure your own family is taken care of. You must put limits on what you give of yourself to people.

As your reputation as a peacekeeper spreads, people will begin to seek you out for help on all manner of things, finding them a job, getting them food. Or they will want to unburden themselves to you like you're a therapist. These types of interactions can be draining and place undue loads on your shoulders. You must learn to say no or limit your response to save your stamina for real peace-keeping duties.

You must also know your limitations—what you can and cannot do. There are times when you are not 100 percent, when you're dealing with other things in your life. There are times when you are not being fair. In these times it is imperative that you hand the baton to a colleague.

Building a network of professional interventionists with similar skills and training is essential so the burden can be shared. This was one of the major reasons I created the Professional Community Intervention Training Institute. Colleagues can put us in check if we become stubborn about pushing forward when common sense dictates we stand down. They form a support group, which provides an outlet for pent-up feelings and a place to recharge batteries. And they can free you up so you have room for other things in your life. I used to feel I had to be everywhere and be everything to all people. If I wasn't there, it wasn't going to get done right. As I matured in the work, I realized training was the key, and once street professionals were trained, I had to believe in my training and let the trainees do their work. I had to believe in my product.

» Finding Family Balance

My wife, Latifah, had a lot of resistance to my intervention work early on in our marriage because she thought I'd get hurt, if not killed. She also believed I was giving a whole lot of myself to unappreciative people and organizations who were taking advantage of my passion to give back. "How many times do the children have to miss out because their father is out saving the world? Our family needs some saving, too," she would say.

I knew I would have to try to explain to Latifah how important this work was to me. I sat her down on the couch one evening. "You have to understand, my sister, this work is my life's mission. I feel I truly found what I've been put here to do. All those years I spent in the life, in the movement, have led me to this work. When I'm able to save lives and keep families from being devastated, that feeling is irreplaceable. When the communities I serve embrace me and bring my team and me into their homes as one of their family, it's matchless. When I see the individuals we serve excel and accept their greatness, it floors me. That's why I do this work. I hope you understand because I won't and can't stop. I love you and this family that I've been blessed to have. All of you are my number one priority, but I also love the people in the communities I serve."

She embraced me with tears in her eyes, and I knew she got it. I never heard another word from her against my intervention work. In fact she has defended it on numerous occasions. Her understanding was a victory. Spouses and families are often not so comprehending because of the amount of time the job takes, the calls in the middle of the night or at the birthday barbecue, the exhaustion that takes over when you do have some home time.

There's no question the family of an interventionist has to put up with a lot. I've had to apologize to my kids because I've snapped at them or been short-tempered due to pressure. I have had the habit of withdrawing into myself and not speaking to anyone if something heavy was going on. I'd spend hours punching the heavy bag in the garage till the house shook, drive iron (lift weights) relentlessly, or practice martial arts to relieve frustration, anger, stress. Now I make sure not to take the street home with me.

When I go home, I'm home. It is my time for my family to take precedence. It was an important boundary to draw, one that finally provided the answer to the question I had asked myself for years: "Am I doing more for people on the street than for my own family?" I am lucky to have such a supportive home life.

My family has always got my back. My wife has not only kept the balance in my life, she's been the rock that has allowed me to do the work. My eldest daughter has often stepped in to help her mother take care of the home front when I've been away; my son-in-law has been like a big brother to my son. My youngest daughter is following my footsteps—she has a degree in criminal justice and has attended my PCITI classes. And I can't forget my six grandkids—their rambunctious antics put a smile on my face and help me unwind at the end of the day.

The key to keeping your sanity is drawing those personal boundaries and sticking to them. It is not selfish—it is the only way you will emotionally survive this work.

» Slipping Back

With their lure of earning easy money, gangs can be powerful magnets. There have been several cases of interventionists who have succumbed to the temptation and fallen back into the life and criminal activity. Their arrests have made sensational headlines, especially if they have been on city contracts. (I am happy to report that no PCITI interventionists have been involved in these cases.) Unfortunately even a few incidents give intervention a bad name and make people think we're just "hug-a-thugs."

Professionalizing intervention through training programs has gone a long way to weed out people ill suited for the work. I give my twenty-week course twice a year, and each time I get a flood of applicants, well beyond the number of students we can accept. The leadership team and myself interview each person, as well as check their reputation on the street. One of the key qualities we look for is the level of the person's commitment.

Some people look at intervention as a way to earn a paycheck. While I definitely believe that intervention specialists need to be paid, and well, I also feel the dollar cannot drive why the peacekeeper does the work. Even if there is no paycheck, the work has to continue as much as the person can do it. The motivation for the work must come from within.

The more insidious danger is from those who haven't really cut their emotional ties to gang life, although they say they have. "We don't get guys to turn them around. They have to really want to change," says PCITI interventionist Saleem El Amin, who's been with me since my days in the Black Power movement.

》Determining Change

The hardest part is ascertaining if the individual really has changed. I have a series of questions and exercises for candidates to determine how deep their gang mindset still is. One of the first things I ask is why they want to change, to look for the source of that personal motivation. The most common reasons are for the sake of their children, the violent death of a close friend or family member, or the risk of going back to prison.

PCITI interventionist Anthony says the death of his twenty-eight-day-old son from Sudden Infant Death Syndrome while he was in prison was instrumental in his turnaround. "I named him Damu—it means 'blood' in Swahili—because I was a Blood. I didn't know it, but I was probably cursing my son. I didn't even get to see my son, to hold him." After Anthony got out, he went through another wild period in the streets, then started thinking about the effect on others. "We started losing kids, innocent bystanders. My mom got shot in the buttocks. It just got stuck on me what was going on."

I also have several exercises I put applicants through. In one of them I bring members of rival sets who have moved away from the life to the applicant interview. If there is resistance from the applicant, I know I've got an issue. Sometimes I have a candidate roll to a rival hood with me and walk the streets. His reaction tells me all I need to know. During the course I assign members of rival gang sets to work together in teams to break down old hostilities.

It's crucial to provide support so people don't slip back into old habits, so I mix a lot of motivational therapy into the lessons. Many of the guys haven't been able to achieve much in life. Their main accomplishments and self-image have resulted from doing things most people would never consider. I have to make them believe they can do good, that they have intrinsic self-worth and that it's not too late to start over.

I drive home the fact that they have to take charge of their communities and families. Real men don't abandon their kids or go around making babies they can't support. They have to be role models for the younger generation and step up to take responsibility, to act with honor and integrity. They can keep their pride in their gang set affiliation, but I hammer on them that they cannot be involved in any way with its vices.

It's not foolproof. I've had dropouts from the course, and even graduates, who have returned to the life. "We see them on the street and they're kind of ashamed," Saleem says. "It's the road of least resistance. They find it hard to readjust. They can't get a job, and the fellows in the hood look up to them. It's easier to do wrong than do right when you don't have a support group. We try to give them that, to reinforce their decisions with positive solutions, but sometimes they're not ready."

The only true way to tell if people are real is by observing their behavior over time to see if they walk the talk. "It was not easy. I can't get high, I can't get in fights, I can't claim a hood," Luis Cardona says. "There are always people who don't understand the power of redemption, of transformation. They're like, 'how do we trust you?' I have to be modeling what I'm telling them."

Interventionists must draw boundaries between their old lives and their new ones, their street lives and home lives, as well as develop reservoirs of personal integrity and resiliency in order to stay true to the mission.

13 PROTOCOLS FOR PEACEKEEPERS: LAYING DOWN RULES AND REGULATIONS

In 1992 the black community's resentment at the lack of respect, opportunity, change, and justice boiled over in Los Angeles. The catalyst was Rodney King.

The case started in March 1991 when police tried to pull King over for speeding. He'd been drinking, and a DUI would've led to a parole violation, so he led cops on a high-speed chase. Five LAPD officers eventually cornered him. During his arrest King was Tasered, hit fifty-six times with batons, and kicked six times. Handcuffed, he was dragged on his stomach to the roadside to wait for an ambulance. He had a fractured facial bone and ankle and numerous cuts and bruises.

The incident was captured on videotape by a nearby resident. Four white officers were charged with use of excessive force and went on trial. As the jury deliberated, everyone knew if the cops got off, all hell was going to break loose. The black community was fed up and furious.

As the trial wound down, I convened an emergency meeting with all my team members to clarify what our responses would be if the streets exploded. We had established procedures, or protocols, for handling all types of violent encounters, but we didn't have the resources or manpower for a mass crisis in the streets, which was exactly what we were expecting.

We went through every possible scenario we could bring forward: random street assaults, group muggings, widespread vandalism, total disregard for any

143

authority, medical-trauma emergencies, and more. We drilled on our responses to each one: Who would be the best people to place at key spots such as major street corners and other gathering spots? What would be their responsibilities? What would be the contingency plans if things went from bad to worse? What resources could we muster up in crisis?

On the day the verdicts were expected, the neighborhoods were tense and fidgety. The jury announced "not guilty" around 3:00 PM, and within minutes the streets turned into a war zone that would last six days.

Our team was in the epicenter of the destruction—burning buildings and trash cans, overturned and vandalized cars, looted stores, smashed windows. Relying on our procedures, we conducted on-the-spot street mediations to halt shootings, removed seniors and children to safe areas, stopped beatdowns, provided support for emergency responders, pulled back people from confronting police officers ready to shoot to kill.

During one particularly overwhelming night, we bumped into another intervention team who wanted to join forces. We were wracked with exhaustion and glad of the offer, so we started talking. I asked them how they worked to determine how we would collaborate. "What's the chain of command in your organization? What's your system for relaying information? How do you handle crowds and move people?"

Their answer was same to every question—"we have relationships." They had no real methods behind their actions, relying instead on their relationships with the homies to handle any situation. I knew we could not use this team in any fashion. They were far more of a liability than an asset. By basing their conduct on pure emotionalism and personalities, they could easily make a misstep that could get someone severely injured or killed. Thanking them for their offer, we explained we would handle what we had to handle. We took a deep breath and plunged back into the chaos, relieved that we had avoided what would have surely resulted in a lot of unnecessary drama.

» Establishing Rules

Protocols—established procedures, strategies, and methods designed for specific situations—set the truly professional interventionists apart from the wannabes. Street credibility and gang culture contacts (LTO) are a key element of intervention, but it alone is not enough. It must be backed by protocols that are proven to be effective, validated through a process of practice, analysis, and practice again. In the world of street violence, errors can get people hurt or terminated. It is essential to minimize mistakes by having protocols that govern behavior.

Before the Professional Community Intervention Training Institute, there had never been a formal operating structure for this work. There were no universally accepted standards of conduct or accountability measures to judge the work. Interventionists simply operated from their gut and the narrow field of their own experience.

I came to realize that standards were needed as more communities, municipalities, and public-safety agencies began to look to community-based intervention as a way to address issues of gangs and violence. Outsiders were intrigued by the concept of using ex-gangsters as peacekeepers, and they had a lot of questions about how it worked, particularly if they were going to fund intervention efforts. Can any ex-gangster be an interventionist? What are the required skills? How do people become interventionists? What are the rules of the game? What do public-safety professionals think of the work? Can this be done elsewhere? How do you know it works?

I saw we had to formalize and professionalize this work with standards if we were to be taken seriously and expand, both on an individual level and the field as a whole. Formalizing also brought more accountability and oversight to the work, which was welcomed by many serious parties such as my team and me. Others, who were basically doing the work for a free paycheck, weren't so embracing. Professionalizing served the need of weeding out those players.

I gave myself the laborious task of coming up with a detailed set of operational and behavioral protocols to guide interventionists and their organizations, much of which has been detailed in this book. Over the years I further found that those protocols really help the interventionists.

» Protocols for Behavior

Understanding street violence, which has its own code of ethics, rules, and logic, has helped save my life on numerous occasions. But the most important factor has been the use of proactive, not reactive, protocols that have enabled me to interpret, control, and ultimately survive crisis situations. It is imperative that professional intervention specialists learn survival thinking and proactive procedures before they hit the streets.

These procedures are the most useful tool the interventionist will have. Knowing what to do will give you the ability to control the engagement and view it with a wider lens that could prevent crisis from turning into catastrophe.

Not knowing what to do, on the other hand, means the interventionist responds reactively, from a defensive position. Acting from this posture you rarely have the ability to manage the encounter because you are constantly playing catch up to what the circumstances dictate.

In crisis situations the average person's first response is to flee or freeze. But interventionists can do neither. They must head directly into the source of violence and work from the inside to extinguish it. It's crucial that interventionists, who never carry weapons, know how to face violence so "fear paralysis" does not take over.

This typically happens when the individual does not have the skills to deal with the impending danger. The person sees it coming and knows something needs to be done, but due to a lack of training or forethought they freeze out of fear.

Fear in itself is good—it is customarily a normal warning sign that the person needs to get out of a situation. But fear can also immobilize you, rob your ability to cope and respond, make you hesitate. This is well known by those who use violence as a means of achieving their goals. They seek to invoke fear and then exploit that freezing reaction to its fullest extent. In the street that is what can get you killed.

Knowing how to confront violent people and situations while minimizing fear is an essential skill for interventionists, who must deal with people who are not only carrying weapons but whose first instinct is to use them. Interventionists have no magic shield; they can easily fall victim to the very violence they are trying to prevent.

Protocols help keep peacekeepers and the people they serve safe from another aspect, too—they limit emotionalism. In situations involving violence, there is no room for emotional thinking. We can never rule out the influence of some emotional bias on our decisions—we are human, but by using protocols, we can control how much emotionalism we let into our actions.

Defining Values

Protocols also govern behavior. They develop an organization's value system, the principles that the group operates by. In violence intervention, having a well-defined value system is essential. Many interventionists are converted ex-gangsters who constantly battle the pull of a world they left behind. Advocating for our clients while trying to steer them from the vices of the gang culture and at the same time navigating around those same vices ourselves becomes a constant journey. Operational and personal behavior protocols serve as buffers to help people stay on the right track. The flow chart below diagrams how it works:

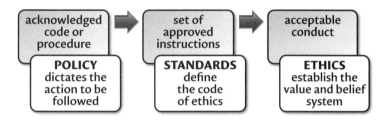

How protocols work

Situations can break down quickly when you are dealing with people who do not possess the same value system. This happened during one of our "Feed the Need" food giveaways.

I had contacted one of our interventionists to arrange a local crew to help unload the semitrailer that we were bringing in to a park in his neighborhood one Saturday. These events usually attract hundreds of people, so we operate them according to strict protocol to keep order and ensure everyone is served. Community members must sign in and form a procession past tables where the food is dropped into each family's shopping bag. Several guys came and started unloading and stacking the food.

Everything was going well until a woman informed me that the local crew was loading the food into shopping carts and wheeling them down the street. I immediately went to the interventionist and told him to check his guys and tell them that was not permitted. The next thing I knew, local gang members arrived, upset. Their wives had called them to complain that the guys at the tables were hiding food behind a tree.

This time I personally stepped to these guys, who got pissed off at being scolded. I then had to mediate with the angry homies to reassure them their

wives would be served, and then I had to calm the crowd, which was starting to get agitated at the unfairness. The whole situation threatened to spin out of control because these guys broke protocols that carried out our fundamental value of equal treatment for everyone.

Developing Protocols

The Los Angeles Fire Department was under attack in a couple neighborhoods. Paramedics were being threatened and insulted, fire apparatus and equipment were being vandalized, certain firefighters were even being stalked. Neither the firefighters nor department leaders could get a fix on why this was happening. Normally someone in the department could get a pulse from the street, but this time they were stuck. The brass called me for help.

I mobilized my team, and we went over the protocols we were going to use. We had to devise some new ones and alter existing ones since this was a unique situation. Usually we're working with two opposing parties. In this instance we didn't know who the opposing party was.

Our first step was to interview the firefighters who appeared to have been personally targeted—some had been followed after responding to emergency calls. The interview process also called for changes in our standard information-gathering process because these guys didn't want to open up at first.

I had to let them know their situation was more precarious than they thought, and eventually they came around. We discovered they had run into the same group of people on several emergency calls. The two parties exchanged words, resulting in these individuals issuing light threats. The firefighters brushed off the threats as "hollow intimidation" and didn't report them.

We then shadowed the firefighters on the job without their knowledge to get an idea as to what was going on. This was a new procedure—we usually didn't evaluate situations unbeknownst to people—but we wanted to see if there was anything in their behavior that had ticked off community members.

We also did a community assessment by conducting "rollouts," street patrols, in the hostile neighborhoods, but we didn't want the community thinking we were accusing them or working for the fire department, so we had to be careful about the questions we asked. Lastly we put word out on the grapevine that we were looking for intel on the firefighter beefs.

After a couple weeks we were able to get to the root of the problem. Seems there was a heated gang war going on involving four major rival sets. The fire department's paramedics were responding to numerous shooting scenes with wounded and dead gang members. Concerned, they started keeping a log tracking who they saw consistently at these scenes to develop profiles of possible shooters.

They soon had a handle on a group of about five suspects. At the next shooting scene several firefighters confronted this group and a verbal altercation took place in front of a crowd of residents and gang members. The group felt the firefighters had blatantly disrespected them in public and set out on a campaign of retaliation that was picked up by others.

We convened a series of sit-downs with the local O.G.'s and explained to them the dire repercussions that would result if any firefighter were injured because of their actions. They reluctantly listened, and with hesitation agreed to allow a "by" on this one, but if firefighters disrespected them again, the pass was off.

We also held training sessions for the firefighters on dealing with the gang mindset. We showed them how to approach gang members and how to talk to them without making them lose face and without putting themselves in jeopardy. Over the following weeks, the threats decreased and finally stopped.

» Procedures and Guidelines

Protocols usually incorporate "standard operating procedures" (SOPs), rarely altered instructions to achieve uniform performance of a specific task, and "standard operating guidelines" (SOGs), recommended but not mandatory courses of action, often a streamlined version of a set practice or sound routine.

The S.T.O.P. formula (Slow down, Think, Observe, Plan) detailed in Chapter 7 is a SOP. This is an inflexible rule that is used in every street situation before you participate in the interaction. A SOG would be interview procedures that change according to the person being interviewed, whether it's the above-referenced firefighters or a grieving mother.

When developing protocols, it's important to keep in mind that interventionists often need to remember and use them in times of stress and tension. For this reason I use simple, easy-to-remember formulas that can be recalled quickly; for instance, the 4W&H formula (who, what, when, why, how) explained in Chapter 7.

Other protocols are generalized concepts that are boiled down to an easy-to-follow outline format.

Steps for Scenario Engagements

Preparing for interaction, the quick, six-point process:

1. **Anticipate the Risk:** Determine the threat factors and risk triggers.

2. **Perceive the Threat:** Develop the ability to see it before it comes, to assess red flags.

3. **Identify Attack Characteristics:** Identify movements and voice patterns of a profile target in specific situations.

4. **Eliminate the Opportunity:** Reinforce comprehensive and practiced procedures.

5. **Implement Beforehand Responses:** Put in place correct standard operating procedures and guidelines.

6. **Debrief, Rewrite, and Redefine SOPs and SOGs:** Analyze all aspects of engagements looking for strong and weak points.

When teaching protocols, presenting them visually is important. As shown in the figure below, simple pictures often stay in students' memories; for example, the Ability-Intent-Opportunity concept, which breaks down violent situations into three fundamental components:

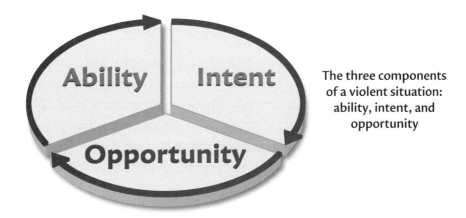

The three components of a violent situation: ability, intent, and opportunity

the perpetrator's "Ability" to use violence and why, his "Intent" to use violence to achieve his goal, and his "Opportunity," his judgment of the target as either an easy mark or someone to be bypassed, usually based on the target's behavior.

This translates into the following protocol:

Intent. Your immediate job is not to figure out the person's intent or to alter his thinking process. Your objective is to secure your safety and bring the person back to normality and stability.

Ability. You have no control over a person's ability to use violence. Don't waste time concentrating on what they can do; focus on what you can do, your ability.

Opportunity. You must control the person's opportunity to use violence. It is crucial that the person does not perceive you as an easy mark or an accessible target. You must display readiness and strength to deal with whatever you're confronted with. Most of your mental and physical energy should be concentrated on marshaling your skills and personal resources to present calm confidence in the face of crisis.

Scenario-Focused, Practitioner-Based Instruction

The most effective training in protocols is developed from scenario-driven, hands-on instruction. This is where students are given real-life situations to handle and physically act out in role-play scenarios. In my PCITI classes, students practice numerous scenarios such as persuading a person brandishing a weapon to put it down, or mediating between armed sets on the street, to name a few.

The exercises should be practiced until students feel comfortable with their ability to manage the encounter. We use a training protocol called "walk through, talk through, run through." The scenario is thoroughly discussed and an action plan developed. Then students go through the action plan at a slow to moderate pace to correct any missteps and make sure they understand the procedure. Finally they run through the procedure at normal speed to see if what they developed is practical.

The goal is to ingrain the procedures as reference points—psychological responses that are automatically retrieved in a crisis. When people are confused, afraid, in doubt, or at a loss, they will resort to a comfort zone that was created in an earlier situation. Having thought-out crisis-management procedures as reference points is a vital survival skill for an interventionist, since responding with emotional, off-the-cuff tactics can be fatal.

Some reference points may be used so often they become deeply ingrained as habitual responses that kick in with little or no thought. While these responses are normally more valuable than not, they can cause you to become complacent or overconfident, which may lead to possibly overlooking other danger signs. Once you have learned procedures, you are ready to go in.

If the protocols were developed correctly, they have been vetted through actual street engagements. They are tried and tested, and tried again. In situations of life and death, you need to be able to make the best judgment calls possible; there is no wiggle room for second-guessing.

Proven options take much of the guesswork out of those calls. Interventionists always want to leave a situation knowing they made the best effort possible with the tools they had available. Protocols are a big part of that.

It is imperative to have a set of formal protocols in professional intervention work. Not only will it formalize and set apart your organization in the eyes of others, it lays out a structure for actions in a field where situations can go awry quickly and the consequences can be grave.

Protocols provide a code of conduct to practitioners who come from a world where the ethical lines are blurry. This book presents a template of common denominator–type protocols that can be adapted for use in any community in any city in any country, but each organization should supplement these with its own protocols tailored to its specific needs and characteristics.

14 THE DEBRIEF: REEVALUATING AND REFINING

A "community empowerment" town hall meeting was taking place at a local community center. Its purpose was unusual—ex-gangsters were asking for atonement and forgiveness from people they had harmed in the past.

The gathering was bringing together O.G.s from rival sets who were now working as peacekeepers, community stakeholders, and local residents, many of whom had lost loved ones at the hands of some of the former gang members they were now facing. From the get-go, it was an emotional meeting, and it quickly spun out of control as victims' relatives seized the opportunity to unleash their anger and grief.

Out of everyone there, one couple stood out. They had lost their sixteen-year-old son two years earlier in a hood assault. No matter what was being said, they just couldn't shake their anger; they didn't seem to understand the goal of the meeting. Everyone was relieved when they left early.

After the session was over, a few of us stayed to discuss how it had gone. We gradually filtered out into the parking lot, still conversing, when gunshots rang out. I felt a hot stab in the back of my leg. Another guy dropped to the ground, yelling in pain. Everyone ran for cover. We had just been shot by the angry couple from the meeting. They had lain in wait in the parking lot to ambush the guy they believed had killed their son. He was left paralyzed. I was more fortunate—the bullet had just torn through the flesh of my right thigh. Everyone else escaped without injury.

The incident was a serious wake-up call. How had we allowed this to happen—how had we not seen something might be coming, given the couple's hard demeanor during the meeting and the fact that they left early but were still in the parking lot after the meeting? We had narrowly escaped death, but I knew we needed to make some hard changes or we might not be so lucky the next time.

I recalled my experience as a militant in the Black Power movement. After every action, we went back to a "war room" in an old storefront and tore down each situation, going over it piecemeal. We had a board, and we'd write up the good moves, the bad ones.

That was what we had to do. We examined the situation and saw our mistakes right away. We did not pay enough attention to the couple's behavior and did not remove the obvious target of their fury. We had allowed them to sit in the parking lot unquestioned, instead of escorting them to their car and pushing them to leave the location. We did not reinforce security around the community center. We came away with several important protocols from that incident including watching people's behavior and securing the premises, inside and out.

I decided we should go further with this process of analysis. We went into lockdown mode in our training room and reviewed five years of street actions. We developed debriefing sheets and a system to score our performance on each situation. We looked at every aspect of our operations—from how team members carried themselves and what they said to specific actions like controlling ingress and egress points. We then built our standard operating procedures based on what our debriefing sheets told us. We also incorporated a debriefing rule in the SOP—after every rollout, we go back to the war room in our headquarters and break down the operation. It has become an essential tool for self-improvement.

》 Situational Debriefing

Debriefing is basically the process of downloading information from an individual about a particular topic. In our work, we use debriefing all the time; to get information at a crime scene, for instance. Situational debriefing is more involved, something akin to a post mortem, with the aim of acquiring information about all the moving parts involved in a past action.

An efficient debriefing process should take place in a quiet location free of interference, preferably with access to a whiteboard, an easel, or overhead projector, anything that can be used to demonstrate actions visually to the group.

The Debriefing Format

The following questions must be answered:

1. Did you meet your established objective? Did the operation go according to plan or was it breached in any way? Were any team members injured? Did any team member break protocol, intentionally or unintentionally?

2. What were the strong and weak points of the event? Why did they work or not work? Do new lesson plans—the specific steps to follow when engaging challenging individuals or occurrences—need to be created or old ones revised? Do these changes require revisions in your SOPs or SOGs?

3. Practice any new SOPs and SOGs through the "talk through, walk through, run through" concept explained in Chapter 7 to determine if there are any flaws. What worked well? What should be improved upon? What should be expanded? Are additional skills needed?

4. Incorporate the SOPs and SOGs in a manual of operation or field manual. This is your "bible" that details your team's tactics, as well as structure.

» Frontal Debriefing

It was a scorching summer afternoon and the air inside the housing project's community room was stifling. The fact that the room was filled to capacity by the residents of the project, as well as the surrounding community, didn't help matters. The meeting had been called to try to quell growing tension between project residents and the cops after a string of fatal police shootings. Officers were getting harassed when they entered the project, and people would run when they saw a patrol car.

At the urging of project residents, the police called us in as community-intervention mediators to help start a dialogue with residents and keep order at a meeting that was sure to be heated. Before accepting the assignment, my team

and I met in the war room and thoroughly broke down all aspects of the event and how we would run it to ensure it remained under control.

We came up with a list of factors that we needed to manage, including controlling the flow of the conversation, arranging the room, setting the time and date of the event, posting our team members as security, and limiting the officers in attendance to those who had a vested interest in the housing project and surrounding patrol area. The police captain agreed.

We scheduled the meeting for a midweek evening so working people could attend and people were less likely to have consumed drugs and alcohol than closer to the weekend. We placed the tables and chairs in a circle so everybody could see each other clearly, did not feel trapped, and had easy access and exit. We controlled the back-and-forth dialogue as a neutral party so it did not turn into a shouting match.

Because our people were securing the event, the police did not need to bring in an overpowering show of force, which could have intensified the anger of some residents and intimidated others. That also relieved the police of worrying about event security, and allowed them to concentrate solely on the meeting.

As predicted, the meeting was explosive as residents vented their frustration and anger, but it remained controlled. The upshot was a plan by police and community leaders to improve relations.

By taking into account all factors beforehand—doing a frontal debriefing—we were able to develop and put into place a plan that managed a situation that could have easily gotten out of hand.

Frontal debriefings are essential when handling events. Although you may have standard operating procedures and guidelines for managing events, each venue and crowd will have its own particular characteristics. A careful advance debrief will allow you to think of details, such as placement of chairs or police presence, tailored to the specific event. Doing so can make all the difference in managing the event successfully.

The debriefing process checks the effectiveness of your training. It lets you know if your manipulative and cognitive skills are working. It provides the opportunity to add, alter, or remove things that don't work. When dealing with crisis situations and violent people, the importance of taking the correct steps cannot be overstressed. Debriefing keeps peacekeepers safe.

15 GOING PRO: DEVELOPING A CORPORATE STRUCTURE

International travel has proved to be an eye-opener to me on the different cultures of violence around the world. I have found many common denominators in violence across continents, but there are also distinctions. Some of the biggest cultural differences I have seen were in China, where we were treated with honor and respect, and I left with great admiration for the people. It was one of the best international experiences I have had doing this work.

We had been invited to China by a coalition of university and community groups to advise them on the urban violence their cities were experiencing. There were some unexpected angles to this violence.

I was walking through the crowded streets of Beijing one afternoon when I heard a commotion behind me. I turned and witnessed a man slapping a woman numerous times, knocking her to the ground. I was stunned, and even more so when he removed his belt and started whipping the woman.

What really shocked me was that no one intervened. People passed by the scene without even a second glance, as if it were a completely normal occurrence. My first instinct was to stop this man, but then I held back. I didn't know this culture or its laws. I had no idea of the parameters I would be stepping into. The man eventually stopped assaulting the woman and hauled her to her feet by her coat. She clung to him, and they walked on like any other couple.

I asked my hosts about this later and was informed that although incidents like this were not typical, domestic violence is a huge problem in China. Sex trafficking is also common, especially in outlying provinces. I was bewildered that women could be openly treated like this in this day and age. I included comprehensive workshops on domestic violence in my agenda.

Another aspect of violence surprised me in China. The government's one-child-only policy has led to a generation of children who are indulged not only by their parents but also by two sets of grandparents. These youths seem to have a sense of entitlement that extends to violent behavior, much of which is learned from music videos—jacking people on trains, assaulting them with knives, etc.

Additionally, because of the premium status that the Chinese family gains from a child's educational achievements, these youths were under major pressure and were snapping mentally, leading to violent outbursts.

This was a unique scenario for me. I'd always dealt with violence bred from poverty, but this was violence resulting from affluence. One of my recommendations was also unusual—kids needed more castigation, which is the last thing I ever advocate, but it was clear to me that these youths needed stricter boundaries and consequences if they violated them. Parents and schools needed to change their priorities and realize the extent of the damage being done to many youths.

My mission to end violence has led to invitations to lend my expertise in some very different societies. I make a point of studying violence everywhere I go. There are different conditions that lead to violence as a response, different factors behind the violence, different circumstances that spur the creation of gangs, but the result is the same—a stifling of human development.

» Professionalizing

My work has steadily progressed through the decades from what was basically an individual mission to disrupt street vices and violence to a group effort that includes working with gangs to working with entire communities. My model for community-based violence intervention has since evolved into a national network and is now gathering momentum as an international movement.

I have had numerous setbacks, but I have always operated from the perspectives of "It's not how you look up, but how you get up," and "Steel sharpens steel"—you have to go through challenge to get to greatness. This mindset has always driven me forward in my mission to end violence. I never looked at this as a way to make money or form a business.

At a certain juncture, though, I saw I had to become more formal and profes-sional or I would not be taken seriously and would miss out on opportunities. This is a whole separate journey for interventionists.

For several decades a core group of us did this work on our own time, on our own dime. To put bread on the table we had to have day jobs and do interven-tion work on the side. But a lot of brothers did not have formal employment, and without compensation for intervention work, they ended up staying connected to the life and its vices of selling drugs, pulling robberies, and so on.

That double life did a real disservice to the work. People couldn't respect in-terventionists when they would see them stopping a major war from erupting in the hood by day and then dealing or using drugs in an alleyway by night.

Things started to change in the late nineties when officials in Los Angeles and a few other cities began looking for alternative ways to stop out-of-control gang violence and related hostility. In Los Angeles, then-City Councilman Tony Cardenas, who is now a congressman, and key staffers Mike Delarosa and Edu-ardo Hewitt, spearheaded a drive to authorize community-based gang inter-vention as an approved city program, allowing resources to be allocated to hire interventionists. (Then City Councilwoman Janice Hahn, Councilman Herb Wesson, and other council members also played major roles in the process.) That was the start of professionalizing the field.

Today there are two main ways of doing intervention work, with pros and cons to each:

1. forming a nonprofit agency
2. subcontracting with an umbrella organization

Setting Up a Nonprofit

When people started asking me if I had a nonprofit, I realized that was the miss-ing link—I had to form a nonprofit, known as a 501c(3) under the federal tax code. Having that nonprofit and knowing how to run it establishes you as a serious, credible player. Organizations feel much more comfortable writing a check to an organization governed by rules and regulations rather than to an individual.

Forming your own nonprofit is the best way to make a living as an inter-ventionist. It operates as a tax-exempt charity, which allows the holder to hold fundraisers and solicit tax-deductible donations as other streams of revenue. It affords you control over how you do your work and provides you with the independence to move forward on your own accord. However, a nonprofit comes with a lot of parameters, and I have seen a lot of individuals trip up on that red tape.

If you file to create a nonprofit, make sure you have a broad statement of purpose that will cover a wide range of services under the organization's umbrella. If you put too narrow a mission, you can get in trouble for carrying out activities that do not relate to the 501c(3)'s purpose. This happens all the time. An individual says her organization was created to promote youth sports, and then she attempts to collect money for ex-offender re-entry housing. It doesn't wash.

Another mistake is not filing an annual tax return. Even though the organization does not pay tax on its revenue, a return must still be filed to show all monies received and how they were spent. Keeping track of money is extremely important. A big error that interventionists make is commingling of funds. Money related to the 501c(3) must be kept separate from other income. If you pay people, you must issue them a 1099 income statement for the year. Most states also require an annual fee and filing to keep the nonprofit as an active concern.

Nonprofits also need boards of directors who serve as the check-and-balance of the organization. It is important you select people you trust and who are wholeheartedly aligned with you and your mission. Even though it is your nonprofit and you are running it, the board will have veto power over decisions that govern the organization's direction. It will also have approval over how much you, as the chief executive, are paid.

Becoming disciplined with tracking your nonprofit income, keeping detailed records, lining up a solid board, and keeping your services aligned with your stated objective are essential to steps to creating a successful nonprofit operation.

Subcontracting

Many interventionists lack the expertise to cope with the business end of the work. A way around that is to subcontract with an established nonprofit organization. Sometimes the organization will simply put interventionists on their payroll.

The advantage to this is that the interventionist does not have to worry about the legalities of maintaining a 501c(3), but the disadvantage is that the agency keeps a portion of any grant money for "administrative oversight" or because they run the show. Moreover, many nonprofits do not pay interventionists fairly, and some also take credit for the interventionists' work, even building a reputation off the peacekeepers' expertise.

It is not that easy to establish a nonprofit status these days. Some interventionists have no choice but to work as subcontractors until they can get their nonprofit filing approved.

❯❯ Sources of Funding

There are two main sources of funding for intervention work: public and private. Public agencies usually award grants on the basis of "requests for proposals" (RFPs), that basically set out what the recipient of the money would do with it. Often there are numerous agencies submitting competing proposals.

RFPs can be complicated to fill out, and attention should be paid to even the smallest requirements such as line spacing and margin width. If those are not adhered to, the applicant will risk having his RFP thrown out.

An important point to remember is that cities commonly require that grantees have a general liability insurance policy to cover anything that might go wrong, and usually the required amount is at least $1 million. If you're conducting training, a second insurance policy for professional liability is required. These policies can add significantly to your overhead costs.

Private funders such as philanthropists and foundations may also require RFPs, but they are not bound by as much red tape as public entities. However they will still want to know how their money is being spent, and careful, detailed paperwork must be kept. If donations are received, receipts must be sent to the donors for tax deduction purposes. A lot of people forget to send receipts, which may cause the donor to think twice about donating the following year.

I have found private funding is the best way to go as it involves less bureaucracy and moves faster. I've had the good fortune to work with several private organizations that have seen the advantages and necessity of community-based violence intervention.

The California Wellness Foundation, in particular its violence prevention division directed by Julio Marcial, has been a strident supporter of the PCITI and has been instrumental in much of our success. A Better LA, an organization led by Coach Pete Carroll, and business executives Bob Hoff, Matt Celenza, and others on the advisory board were key early supporters of ours, putting the first privately funded interventionists on the street and launching the PCITI.

Both A Better LA and The California Wellness Foundation continue to be vital partners in our growth, and my relationships with their principals have evolved from business partnerships to personal friendships. I have to personally salute A Better LA and A Better Seattle. Those organizations have done more to support hard-core community intervention and restoration in those cities than most organizations in this line of work. Their executive and advisory boards have been instrumental in assisting both myself and the PCITI, allowing us to make many of the strides we have been fortunate to accomplish.

In order to find out about available grants and RFPs, as well as to establish their reputations, interventionists must make contacts beyond their traditional comfort zone. Sometimes personnel at a granting agency will contact people they know to ask them to submit an RFP.

Building networks of contacts is key, especially as grants vary from year to year. If you get a grant one year, there's no guarantee that you'll get it the following the year or if it will be offered again. Funding is always up and down, depending on municipal budgets and local politics.

» Street Expertise vs. Academic Study

An irony of intervention work is that interventionists are hired for their street smarts—their contacts and experience. That's their expertise. They don't generally have a lot of formal education. But grants are often awarded to RFPs written by academics whose expertise is grant writing by organizations that have the resources to file slick presentations. That paradox has led to a lot of interventionists being unfairly overlooked for many grants and has also hurt the community the money is supposed to help.

Many of these organizations have little expertise or knowledge related to the people and culture they are being hired to interact with. Some of them create procedures, which have never been tested and validated, just to demonstrate that some work was accomplished.

The result is that when these grants run out, nothing has been effectively put into place. These organizations pack up and leave the community in a worse state than before.

To prevent this from happening, professional interventionists must assume the responsibility to learn how to do the business side of the work. This can be done by finding allies who truly believe in the cause and can mentor you.

Another step in professionalization is having your work validated by outside experts. University of California, Los Angeles, professor of social welfare Jorja Leap has evaluated the PCITI and made valuable suggestions over the years, as has Angie Wolf, senior researcher from the National Council on Crime & Delinquency.

Debra Warner has been instrumental in providing psychological expertise, while other university experts, including Robert Hernandez and Billie Wise, have also given us the platform of their validation. Journalist and author Celeste Fremon and James Bolden have helped us to tell our story.

» National Expansion

As community-based violence intervention has become increasingly recognized, my work has expanded far beyond California. In past decades I worked in community-violence intervention and gang prevention from coast-to-coast for organizations including Youth Gang Services, the Rand Corp., MAD DADS, and the National Association of Blacks in Criminal Justice.

In more recent years I have partnered with organizations around the country to establish regional alliances and gang-intervention certification programs. Using the PCITI template, manual, and protocols, these programs have trained and certified hundreds of street peacekeepers, as well as peacekeeper instructors, emergency responders, educators, graduate students, social-service specialists, and mental-health professionals in the District of Columbia, Baltimore, Virginia, Tacoma, and other cities. In Seattle we developed a community safety response team in addition to training gang outreach workers. We have also helped develop think tanks in cities including Chicago and Oakland.

We have been fortunate to have had partners, both public and private, who have teamed up with us and often funded this work: A Better Seattle, the Seattle Seahawks, Seattle Alive and Free, the Seattle YMCA, the City of Seattle, the City of Tacoma Mayor's Office, the Columbia Heights/Shaw Collaborative and the

DC Children & Youth Trust Investment Corp. in the District of Columbia, as well as the following public agencies: the U.S. Department of Justice's Office of Justice Programs, Office of Juvenile Justice and Delinquency Prevention; Maryland's Montgomery County Department of Health and Human Services; and Prince George's County Department of Social Services.

I am constantly fielding inquiries by other cities requesting my consulting services and training expertise on gang, violence, and public-safety issues. The movement grows.

» Global Violence

El Salvador is one of the most murderous countries in the world. Driving that violence is the rivalry between two major gangs: the Mara Salvatrucha (MS-13) and the 18th Street gang. On their own accord, the two gangs declared a truce in 2012. In 2013 I was one of a delegation of eleven U.S. experts—and the only non-Latino—invited by the gangs to substantiate the truce, which was being viewed skeptically by the government, and to inspect prison conditions. We paid our own expenses in order to keep our neutrality.

We went into all seven gang prisons in the country to interview inmates. Their living conditions were deplorable—grossly overcrowded, unsanitary bathing and toilet facilities, even rats and dirt floors. I ran into a number of gang members I had known in L.A. who had been deported to El Salvador.

We also met for four hours with major shot callers on the street, who assured us they were real about the truce, which they had called for many reasons. One that stood out—they wanted the next generation to have a chance at a better life and to lessen the pain violence has inflicted on so many families. Additionally they hoped the truce would motivate the government to improve prison conditions.

Government officials heard we were visiting and asked to meet us. We held sessions with authorities from several departments. At the end of the visit a report was written and sent to the appropriate authorities in Washington and El Salvador. Our delegation remains in contact with people in El Salvador—the last we heard was the truce was still holding strong.

I only hope that prison conditions will improve and the truce will gain more support from the government and community. Ending violence is an essential first step to improving living standards, whether in a Salvadoran pueblo or a Chicago housing project. I have seen it time and again—violence chokes communities like weeds choke gardens; nothing can grow when violence dominates.

Many of my overseas trips, including those to China, Egypt, and Ghana, have involved teaching community intervention and empowerment techniques. In Ghana, another country where we were treated like royalty, I also did a self-motivation workshop for five hundred children in a number of schools that had no books, located in villages without running water. Ghana was an instance where I saw a different attitude toward law and order. The Ghanaian police, actually soldiers armed with M-16s, were on the point of arresting us for taking photos of a university until our host intervened. I later sat down with the officers and we discussed rules and policies in their respective countries. I learned that they were sensitive about their university because they valued it highly and had seen its treasures taken by foreigners in the past. Communication and comprehension is key in overcoming cultural barriers.

I have also trained police agencies abroad. In Peru, Argentina, and Brazil, where they rolled out the red carpet for our organization, we trained SWAT teams and police and fire personnel in techniques to deal with street violence and crisis intervention. We also consulted for Scotland Yard detectives in London about urban violence.

International groups have visited us at home. A community antiviolence group from Sweden, the Back Up team, has come twice to Los Angeles for peacekeeper training and has invited us to go there for further training. We've also hosted community groups from El Salvador and police from London.

All these contacts with different groups and countries have enriched and broadened my work. Every time a group contacts me, whether from within the United States or outside, it is a sign that comprehensive, professionally driven intervention work is becoming an increasingly accepted part of the global solution to violence.

I don't pretend to have all the answers, but I offer a way for communities to take charge of their own destinies, to stand up against the scourge of violence. I am firmly convinced that if each of us does our part, we can truly make an impact and reduce violence to a minimum so people can live healthy and productive lives, which is what every human being deserves.

We move forward with the work. Peace out.

Glossary of Gang Slang

AR-15: semiautomatic assault rifle

barrio: Spanish for neighborhood. *See also* hood, neighborhood

beef: problem, misunderstanding

behind the wall, the pen: incarcerated

big bro: respected elder, mentor

blast: shoot

bling, glitters: jewelry

bumperjack: automotive jacks used as street weapons

buster: person claiming a reputation or credibility he does not have

cannon: shotgun, rifle

cherried out: in peak condition

click, clique, clica (Spanish): localized gang with geographic boundaries, a gang subset

double O.G., triple O.G.: gang member with two or three generations of family members in the gang

fool: sucker, chum, idiot

fronting: loud talking, faking, bluster

game, the: gang culture, prostitution, drug selling

hardcore: ability to carry out the extreme actions

homie, homeboy: gang member, buddy

hood, neighborhood: geographic location claimed by a gang

intel: information

jacked: robbed, stolen

jacket: criminal record

jump-in: beating to gain gang membership

jump-out: beating to gain permission to leave a gang

mad-dogging, staredown: staring disrespectfully, with the intention to intimidate, challenge

Mini-14: small, semiautomatic rifle

O.G.: original gangster, veteran gang member with clout

pad: home

paper: money

popo: law enforcement, police

popped: arrested

punked: totally disrespected

put in work: injure rivals

roll: move into action

safebanging: using social media for gang warfare

set: localized gang with geographic boundaries, segment of a larger gang

shot caller: gang leader with credibility, decision maker

shredded: muscular physique

slinging: street drug dealing

soldier: gang member

stand-down: hold off, back off

strawberry: prostitute paid in drugs

tag: graffiti signifying a gang

tat: tattoo worn to indicate gang membership

throwdown: physical, verbal ability to confront challenges, back up your word

wasted: killed, usually intentional

Index

A

Ability-Intent-Opportunity protocol, 151
acknowledgment signs, 43
affiliates, 24
affluence, 160
afterschool programs, 102, 121
aggression, 90, 118, 134
alcohol: as aggression factor, 111; grieving and, 80, 85; as self-medication, 100; as violent behavior risk factor, 87, 88, 89, 92, 95–96
Alive & Free program, 12
altered level of consciousness (ALC), 95–96
anger, 124, 134
arbitration, 71
Asian gangs, 22, 23, 30, 43–44
assessing a crisis, 90–91
associates, 24
atonement, 137, 154
attitude change, 14, 110–112, 130

B

Back Up team, 168
Basheer, Amir, 115–116
Basheer, Latifah, 112–114, 138–140
bathrooms, 107
beatings, as initiations, 22
Beck, Charles, 10
Behind the Wall, 127–128
belonging, 20
betrayal, 21
Better LA, A, 41, 164
Better Seattle, A, 41, 164
black gangs, 22, 23, 43–44
Black Power movement, 41–42, 54, 155

blame, 59–60, 76
Bloods, 23, 33–35, 42
body language, 39, 90
Bolden, James, 165
boundaries, setting, 137–138, 140, 160
Boys and Girls Club, 102
Brotherhood Unified for Independent Leadership through Discipline (B.U.I.L.D.), 121
Brother II Brother, 82
Brown, Stinson, 82–84
bullying, 29
Burton, Brent, 50–51
busters, 37

C

California Peace Prize, 15
California Wellness Foundation, 163–164
Cambodian gangs, 42–44
candlelight vigils, 80
Cardenas, Tony, 161
Cardona, Luis, 124, 137, 142
Carroll, Pete, 40–41, 164
ceasefires, 5, 7, 13, 68, 69
Celenza, Matt, 164
channeling, 53
children: Chinese reproduction policies and culture of, 160; codes of honor regarding, 22; as drive-by victims, 46, 77–78, 135; of interventionists, 138–140; off-limit declarations regarding, 7; of prisoners, 134; school shootings, 58–59; sexual abuse of, 108–109. *See also* schools
China, 159–160
Chow, Mark, 86
churches, 82

clicks, 25, 30
clothing, 23, 51–52, 110, 118
codes of honor, 22–23
colors, 23, 118
commitment, 12, 41, 88, 136, 144
communication: conflict assessments and, 90–91; to contacts on engagement details, 89; crime-scene management and information dispersal, 51–52; for cultural understanding, 167; mediation, 5–6, 36–38, 66–74; rumor control, 48, 52–53, 58–65; victim engagement and, 76–78
communities: crime-scene management and liaison with, 48; empowerment and restoration of, 98–104; ex-gangsters and forgiveness requests from, 154; gang presence impact on, 9, 10, 167; mobilization efforts, 8–9, 25, 120–121; town hall meetings, 98–99, 166–168; trauma exposure statistics, 100. See also neighborhoods
Communities in Schools, 124–125
Community Incident Safety Response Team, 103
compromise, 114
conflict resolution, 5–6, 36–38, 66–74
congregation prohibitions, 25, 30
contacts and backups, 61–62, 89, 138
Cooper, Kwame, 50, 57
counseling, 107, 111–112, 130, 132
covers, 89
crews, 24
crime-scene management: crowd control, 50–53; information and situation assessments to first responders, 50; law enforcement at, 14, 47–48, 53–55; paramedics and firefighters at, 55–57; personal observation and documentation at, 2–4, 52–53, 61; rumor control, 52–53, 58–62; street trauma first aid, 48–50; victims' family members, 75–77; zones of, 51
Crips, 23, 33–35, 42
crowd control, 50–53

D

De, Nikko, 49–50
death, 21–22, 25–26, 51, 88–89, 97
debriefing, 155–158
Delarosa, Mike, 161
denial, 76, 117

depersonalization, 25–26, 125
deportation, 30–31
disappointment, 136–137
discrimination, 54, 56
disrespect, 26–27, 31, 50–51, 52, 149–150
Division of Juvenile Justice and Delinquency Prevention (U.S. Department of Justice), 12
domestic violence, 28, 75, 79, 105–114, 159–160
drills, scenario-driven, 123
drive-by shootings, 46–48, 77–78, 135
drugs: gang culture of, 1–2, 6, 42; grieving and, 80, 85; as self-medication, 100; as violence risk factor, 87, 88, 95–96, 106, 111

E

economic discrimination, 56
education, 28
18th Street gang, 166
El Amin, Saleem, 140–141, 142
elderly people, 22, 66
El Salvador, 30–31, 166–167
emotion, 60, 93–95, 106, 146
emotional toll, 75–77, 85, 135–142
empathy, 25–26, 76
employment, 10, 28, 39–40, 98–99, 129–130
encirclement, 53
enforcers, 24
enhancements, 30
entitlement, 160
exit points, 90, 91
exit rituals, 31
eye movements, 90

F

facilitation, 71
families: codes of honor regarding, 22; domestic violence, 28, 75, 79, 105–114, 159–160; for domestic-violence support, 107; gang tradition in, 20, 24, 110–111, 117; incarceration-intervention programs supporting, 128, 132, 134; of interventionists, 138–140; postprison reconnection with, 128–129. See also survivors as victims
Fathers Involved in Redefining Men (F.I.R.M.), 121
fear: as gang-control tactic, 4, 9, 22, 28, 146; interventionists' management of, 146; mediation viewed as sign of, 67, 69

"Feed the Need," 86–87, 147–148
fight-or-flight syndrome, 100, 146
fights, 79, 87, 109–110
firefighters: attacks on, 148–150; at crime
    scenes, 46–48, 50–52, 55–57; diversity hir-
    ing policies, 57; economic-discrimination
    and victim-treatment issues, 56, 57; first
    responders' street-survival training for, 57
fire stations, as safe houses, 121
food giveaway programs, 86–87, 147–148
forgiveness, 83
Fremon, Celeste, 165
funding, 81, 161, 163–164
funerals, 33–35, 78, 80–82
funneling, 53

G

gangs, overview: average age at joining, 20;
    criminal businesses of, 10; cultural com-
    ponents of, 26–28; depersonalization of,
    25–26; domestic violence reinforced by
    mentality of, 111; factors supporting, 10; fate
    acceptance, 21; formation factors and char-
    acteristics, 22; geographic locations, 24–25;
    growth and expansion of, 10–11; hierarchies
    within, 23–24; identification methods, 23;
    initiation rites for, 22; intellect and street
    savvy, 28; law enforcement and, 29–31; leav-
    ing, 31–32; membership justification and
    motivation, 19–21, 26–28, 125; recruiting
    strategies, 115–117; rules and code of honor,
    22–23; violent personalities of, statistics, 28
Ghana, 167
girls. *See* women/girls
gladiator syndrome, 124
graffiti, 25, 102
Grape Street Crips, 25
"green light," 31, 44
grief, 82–85
Griffith, Penny, 109–110
groupies, 24
guilt, 76, 84, 85, 134, 135, 136

H

Hahn, Janice, 161
halfway houses, 129
handshakes, 19
healing circles, 124
Hernandez, Robert, 100, 165

Hewitt, Eduardo, 161
hierarchies, 23–24, 72, 118
hits, 31, 44
Hoff, Bob, 164
Honduras, 30
hoods, 1–2, 39–41, 61. *See also* turfs
hospitals, 78–80
houses, and safety precautions, 107
houses of worship, 82
human trafficking, 10

I

immediate danger to life (IDL) areas, 51
impact sessions, 101, 121, 130
initiation rites, 22
injunctions, gang, 25, 30
insurance, 163
integrity, 34, 41, 44, 141
intellect, 28
intent (violent situation component), 151
international movements, 160, 166–168
Internet, 30
intervention, overview: early law enforce-
    ment rejection of, 14, 47–48; goals of, 9;
    job description examples, 1–9, 15–17; law-
    enforcement partnership with, 14–15; as life
    calling, 137; professionalizing, 12–15, 144,
    160–168; protocol development for, 143–
    152; rewards of, 137, 138; street expertise *vs.*
    academic study, 164–165; training courses
    and programs for, 12–14, 57, 164
interventionists (peacekeepers): contacts and
    networking support, 61–62, 89, 138; deaths,
    88–89, 97; emotional toll on, 75–77, 85,
    135–136; family balance, 138–140; felony
    records restricting activities of, 122; gang-
    life temptations, 140, 141–142, 147, 161;
    law-enforcement relationships with, 14–15,
    48, 53–55; negotiation roles and guidelines,
    70, 71; as role models, 125, 141, 142; safety
    strategies, 7; skills and qualities of, 11–14,
    72–73, 140–142 (*see also* LTO); street-savior
    syndrome and coping strategies, 137–140
investigation response teams, 62
isolation, 53, 132

J

jealousy, 109–110
Jett, Barbara, 110

Johnson, Magic, 39–40
judgment, 11, 32, 70, 95, 108
jump-ins, 22
jump-outs, 31
juvenile correction facilities, 132–133

K

killings, categories of, 4
King, Rodney, 14, 69, 143–144
kitchens, 107

L

Latino gangs, 22, 23, 30, 43–44
law enforcement: civilian abuse and deaths
    by, 16–17, 143–144; crime-investigation
    inefficiency and community response, 8;
    at crime scenes, 48, 50–51, 53–55; distrust
    of, 50–51, 54; early violence intervention
    and response from, 14, 47–48; as funeral
    patrols, 82; gang-control methods, 25, 29–
    30; harassment and shooting of, 156–158;
    intervention effectiveness of, 10; interven-
    tionist relationships with, 14–15, 48, 53–
    55, 167
Leap, Jorja, 165
license to operate. *See* LTO
lifestyle of gangs, 20, 125
limitation awareness, 138
lists, gang member, 30
location assessments, 89–90
Los Angeles County, 10, 23–24, 30, 41, 161
Los Angeles Unified School District, 120
loyalty, 22, 23, 38
LTO (license to operate, street credibility):
    acquisition of, 38–41; description and
    overview, 35–36; as interventionist require-
    ment, 11, 36–38; loss of, 42, 55; maintaining,
    41–42; as mediation requirement, 72–73;
    outsider collaborations and, 44–45; types of,
    43–44

M

mad-dogging, 5, 35, 39, 43
Mara Salvatrucha (MS-13), 166
Marcial, Julio, 163–164
McDowell, Yvette, 81
mediation, 5–6, 36–38, 66–74
mentoring programs, 82, 128, 132–133
money, 19, 28, 106. *See also* funding

N

negotiations, 5–6, 36–38, 66–74
neighborhoods, 1–2, 39–41, 61. *See also* turfs
networking, 61–62, 138, 164
neutrality, 72
nonprofit organizations, 161–162
Northwest Leadership Foundation, 12

O

O.G.s (original gangsters), 23–24
opportunity (violent situation component),
    151
opportunity killings, 4
outsiders, 38–41, 43, 45, 64, 100

P

paramedics, 46–47, 50, 51–52, 55–56, 57
parents, 21, 43–44, 117, 130, 134
parks, 8, 10, 30, 71, 100, 102
patience, 72, 107, 114
PCITI. *See* Professional Community Interven-
    tion Training Institute
peacekeepers. *See* interventionists
peace talks, 5–6, 36–38, 66–74
peer pressure, 20
permanence, 23
personal involvement, 93–95
personal killings, 4
personal space violations, 90, 91
police. *See* law enforcement
Police Athletic League, 102
poverty, 10, 20, 160
power, as gang-membership motivation, 20, 28
prestige, 28
pride symbolism, 23
prison, 21, 23, 31, 38, 126–134, 166–167
Professional Community Intervention Training
    Institute (PCITI): candidate assessments and
    selection, 140–142; development of, 12, 41;
    expertise evaluation and program validation,
    165; food giveaway programs of, 86–87, 147–
    148; funding sources, 163–164; international
    partnerships, 159–160, 166–167; national
    expansion of, 165–166; for networking and
    support, 138; protocol development for pro-
    fessionalization, 145; protocol instruction
    strategies, 145–151
professionalization: business types, 161–163;
    challenges to, 164–165; for credibility, 144,

161; funding sources, 163–164; program development, 11–15; program evaluation and expertise validation, 165; protocols for, 87–88, 144–151

prostitution, 1, 10, 95–96

protection, as gang-membership motivation, 19

protocols: benefits of, 145–148; debriefings and revisions to, 156; procedural examples, 150–151; professionalization and need for, 144–145; situation-based development of, 148–150; training strategies for, 151, 152

public-safety assistants, 102–103

R

race, as gang characteristic, 22

racism, 54

rational thinking, 90, 92–95

recidivism, 128, 129, 130

redemption, 137, 142

relationship killings, 4

reputation, 4, 27, 36, 44

requests for proposals (RFPs), 163, 164

respect: acknowledgment showing, 43; funerals as, 33; as gang cultural value and membership motivation, 19, 25–27, 26, 38; retaliation to maintain, 7; stand-downs at funerals for, 34; street credibility earned through, 26

response zones, 91–92

responsibility claims, 4–5

retaliation. *See* revenge/retaliation

revenge killings, 4

revenge/retaliation: at candlelight vigils, 80; at funerals, 33, 81; as gang cultural component, 27; at hospitals, 79; intervention strategies to control, 66, 77, 85, 101 (*see also* mediation); motives for, 3–4, 4, 7, 60, 149; wasting time on, 127

revenue, 28. *See also* funding

review and revisit, 27–28

riots, 143–144

risk assessments, 87–89

Rivers, T Top, 125, 137

robberies, 4, 10

Rodriguez, Blinky, 78, 84, 124–125, 137

Rodriguez, Lilly, 84

Rogers, T, 39

role modeling, 125, 141

rollouts (street patrols), 101, 149, 155

rumor control, 48, 52–53, 58–65

S

safebanging, 30

safe houses, 121

"safe passage" programs, 120

safety drills, school, 123

safe zones, 69

schools: community response teams for, 121–122; community-restoration and after-school programs, 102; disciplinary policies of, 124; empowerment programs at, 8; gang infiltration in, 115–119; gang protection from bullying at, 29; low-quality, as gang membership factor, 28; one-on-one intervention in, 123–125; safe-house system, 121; safe-passage programs, 120; as safe zones, 69, 121; shootings at, 58–60, 122–123; youth programs at, 121

Scotland Yard, 167

scouts on post, 120

Seattle, WA, 12, 41, 102–103, 164, 165

Seattle Seahawks, 12, 102

Seattle Youth Violence Initiative, 12, 102

self-esteem, 20, 25, 101

7 R's of gang culture, 26

sex trafficking, 1–2, 10, 95–96, 159–160

sexual abuse, 108–109

shelters, domestic violence, 107

shooters, 24

shot callers, 24, 33, 36–38, 81

showdowns. *See* street crises

slang, 118

"smile now, cry later" philosophy, 23

snitching, 22, 23, 38, 42, 54

sociopathy, 24

soldiers, 24

solidarity, 20

sports activities, 102, 124–125

staging, 46–47, 50

stance, 39, 90

standard operating guidelines and procedures (SOGs and SOPs), 150, 156

stand-downs, 5, 7, 34, 37–38, 44, 68, 69

staredowns, 5, 35, 39, 43

Stentorians, 57

S.T.O.P. formula, 89–92, 150

street credibility. *See* LTO

street crises: community restoration and prevention of, 101; description, 87; at food giveaway events, 86–87, 147–148; intervention
planning and preparation, 89; management
strategies for, 89–92; personal involvement
in, 93–95; rational thinking and calmness requirements, 92–93; risk-factor assessments,
87–89; substance abuse as risk factor for,
95–96; threats and safety strategies, 96–97
street patrols, 101, 149, 155
street-savior syndrome, 137–140
stress, 68, 75–77, 76, 136
structure, as gang membership motivation, 19
subcontracting, 162–163
suicide, 9, 29, 59, 77, 84–85
survivors as victims: assistance to, overview,
75–76, 85; candlelight vigils, 80; coping
with loss, 82–84; and emotional toll, 76–77,
85; funeral-attendance restrictions, 80–81,
82; funeral safety, 81; at hospitals, 78–80;
suicide, 9, 84–85; victim engagement and
assistance, 77–78
Sweden, 168

T

tags, 25
tattoos, 23
taxes, 71, 100, 162
Taylor, Bo, 40–41
teachers, 116–119, 122–123, 133
teardrop motifs, 23
tents, forensic, 52
threats, 96–97
throwdowns, 24, 27, 36
town hall meetings, 98–99, 166–168
trauma exposure, 100
trials, 77–78
truces, 13, 69, 166–167
trust, 36, 44, 100
turfs, 24–25, 34–35, 38–39, 72, 81

V

value systems, 26, 147
victim engagement, 76–78

victims: of domestic violence, 75, 105–106,
107–110; drive-by shootings, 46–48, 77–78,
135; forensic tents and respect of, 52; gang
family members, 1–9; at hospitals, 78–80;
identification assistance, 52; school shootings, 58–60. *See also* survivors as victims
violence, overview: in China, 159–160; code of
honor restrictions on, 7, 22–23; community
restoration and reduction of, 101–102; community *vs.* gang, comparisons, 101; crime-
scene descriptions, 2–3; economic factors,
10, 20, 160; gang justification of, 3–4, 7, 26,
28; traditional prevention strategies, 9; violence linked to, 8. *See also related topics*

W

wannabes, 24
Warner, Debra, 129, 130, 165
war rooms, 62, 155
weapons, 5, 6, 72, 82, 88, 89
Wesson, Herb, 161
white gangs, 22
Who, What, When and How (4W&H) risk
formula, 87–88, 150
Williams, Mike, 98–99
Wolf, Angie, 165
women/girls: and domestic violence, 105–114,
159–160; as gang members for protection,
28–29; jealousy over men, 110; off-limit
declarations, 7; self-esteem issues, 110
Women Improving Neighborhoods (WIN), 110
Woodle, Curtis, 52, 54, 60

Y

youth programs, at-risk, 12, 101, 102, 121,
123–125

Z

zones: community restoration and neighborhood safe, 101; immediate danger to life
(IDL), 51; neutral, for mediation, 72; off-
limits, 82; response, 91, 92; school safe, 123;
segregation at schools, 118